EUL VERLAG

QUANTITATIVE ÖKONOMIE

Herausgegeben von Prof. Dr. Eckart Bomsdorf, Köln, Prof. Dr. Wim Kösters, Bochum, und Prof. Dr. Winfried Matthes, Wuppertal

Band 155
Ronald Franken
Support-Vektor-Maschinen und statistische neuronale Netze im Data Mining und Datenqualitätsmanagement – Eine empirische Analyse am Beispiel der Unternehmenssolvenz
Lohmar – Köln 2008 • 348 S. • € 63,- (D) • ISBN 978-3-89936-756-0

Band 156
Dana Schüler
Macroeconomic and Microeconomic Effects of Migration
Lohmar – Köln 2009 • 236 S. • € 56,- (D) • ISBN 978-3-89936-769-0

Band 157
Christoph Scheicher
Armut, Reichtum, Umverteilung: Begriff und statistische Messung
Lohmar – Köln 2009 • 184 S. • € 48,- (D) • ISBN 978-3-89936-808-6

Band 158
Karl-Kuno Kunze
Persistenz und Antipersistenz im deutschen Aktienmarkt – Eine empirische Untersuchung
Lohmar – Köln 2009 • 256 S. • € 57,- (D) • ISBN 978-3-89936-811-6

Band 159
Martin Noppenberger
Kostenminimierung in Speichernetzwerken
Lohmar – Köln 2009 • 248 S. • € 56,- (D) • ISBN 978-3-89936-862-8

Band 160
Elisabeth Meyer
New Perspectives on the Role of Information in Health Economics
Lohmar – Köln 2009 • 160 S. • € 47,- (D) • ISBN 978-3-89936-864-2

JOSEF EUL VERLAG

New Perspectives on the Role of Information in Health Economics

Inaugural-Dissertation
zur Erlangung des Grades
Doctor oeconomiae publicae (Dr. oec. publ.)
an der Ludwig-Maximilians-Universität München

vorgelegt von
Elisabeth Meyer

Referent: Prof. Ray Rees
Korreferent: Prof. Dr. Mathias Kifmann
Promotionsabschlussberatung: 04. Februar 2009

Reihe: Quantitative Ökonomie · Band 160

Herausgegeben von Prof. Dr. Eckart Bomsdorf, Köln, Prof. Dr. Wim Kösters, Bochum, und Prof. Dr. Winfried Matthes, Wuppertal

Dr. Elisabeth Meyer

New Perspectives on the Role of Information in Health Economics

EUL VERLAG

Bibliografische Information der Deutschen Nationalbibliothek

Die Deutsche Nationalbibliothek verzeichnet diese Publikation in der Deutschen Nationalbibliografie; detaillierte bibliografische Daten sind im Internet über <http://dnb.d-nb.de> abrufbar.

Dissertation, Ludwig-Maximilians-Universität München, 2009

ISBN 978-3-89936-864-2
1. Auflage November 2009

JOSEF EUL VERLAG GmbH
Brandsberg 6
53797 Lohmar
Tel.: 0 22 05 / 90 10 6-6
Fax: 0 22 05 / 90 10 6-88
E-Mail: info@eul-verlag.de
http://www.eul-verlag.de

Bei der Herstellung unserer Bücher möchten wir die Umwelt schonen. Dieses Buch ist daher auf säurefreiem, 100% chlorfrei gebleichtem, alterungsbeständigem Papier nach DIN 6738 gedruckt.

Acknowledgements

First of all, I would like to thank my supervisor, Professor Ray Rees, for his support and encouragement. He is also the co-author of the study in Chapter 4 of this thesis, and I am grateful for the chance to collaborate with him on this topic. Moreover, as the head of the *Seminar für Versicherungswissenschaft*, he always managed to create a pleasant work atmosphere and to keep the non-scientific workload as low as possible. Equally, I am indebted to my second supervisor, Professor Mathias Kifmann. I greatly benefitted from his comments on my papers and from various discussions I had with him. He invited me on several occasions to the University of Augsburg to attend seminars and present my own work, which I found very helpful. Moreover, I thank Professor Reiner Leidl, who kindly agreed to join the board of referees for this thesis.

For excellent comments and suggestions concerning my research work, I am indebted to Konstantin Beck, Michael Kuhn, Normann Lorenz, Florian Mamberer, Maximilian Rüger and Clarissa Schnekenburger. My colleagues Florian Englmaier and Ingrid Königbauer were always available to discuss new research ideas at an early stage. Moreover, I would like to thank my colleagues Tobias Böhm, Arno Schmöller, Astrid Selder and Hans Zenger for good cooperation. Special thanks go to Irmgard von der Herberg and Silke Englmaier for their support in all administrative matters, and to Dirk Rösing for excellent IT support. I would also like to mention our student helpers Florian Bitsch, Kinga Funk, Catharina von Liel and Maximilian von Liel.

My work has benefitted from comments by seminar participants at the University of Munich, the 6th and 7th European Health Economics Workshop (2006, 2007), the Annual Meeting of the *Verein für Socialpolitik* (2006, 2007), the 6th European Conference of the International Health Economics Association (iHEA,

2006), the 6th World Congress of the iHEA (2007) and the European Science Days in Steyr (2007, 2008).

This thesis project was supported by the German Science Foundation within the research training group *Markets, Institutions and the Scope of Government*, which I gratefully acknowledge.

Most importantly, however, I am indebted to my parents, who have encouraged and supported me throughout my life, and to Frank, who has made the last years special.

Munich, October 2009 Elisabeth Meyer

Contents

Chapter 1

Introduction

1.1 Motivation

Problems of asymmetric information are so prevalent in the health care sector that they can be said to characterize this market.[1] Already Arrow (1963) points out the main problems existing in the market for health care services. Firstly, when patients are fully insured against health care costs, they demand treatment even if the benefit from it is lower than the cost. Traditional health insurance controls this moral hazard with consumer copayments. However, proportional cost reimbursement by the insurer still works as a price subsidy for medical goods and services at the margin, encouraging an inefficient use of these goods. Essentially, as Arrow notes, the market failure lies in the non-contractibility of the consumer's true health status. A first-best insurance policy would specify a fixed payment contingent on health, which would leave the patient's health care demand undistorted.

This phenomenon of ex post moral hazard[2] is characteristic for the contracts between health insurers and consumers. The second problem which Arrow mentions concerns the physician-patient relationship. Clearly, this relationship is characterized by severe informational asymmetries. Physicians are uniquely qualified to make a diagnosis and provide treatment. Due to the lack of information, patients are often unable to assess the quality and appropriateness of treatment, even in ret-

[1] See also Gaynor (1994).

[2] See Zeckhauser (1970), Ma and Riordan (2002) for a formal analysis.

rospect. Physicians may be able to "induce" demand for services which the patient would not desire under full information, or to charge for services which have not been provided. Health insurance exacerbates these problems because it reduces the patient's financial incentive to monitor the physician.[3]

In recent years, the share of health care expenditure in GDP has been rising rapidly in virtually all developed countries. In Germany, for example, this proportion has more than doubled, rising from 4.7% in 1960 to 10.6% in 2006. This is currently the fourth highest value of all OECD nations. The United States rank first in this statistic with a share of 15.3% in 2006 (up from 4.8% in 1960).[4] Of course, informational asymmetries cannot be the main driving force behind the *growth* in expenditure, because these problems have always been existing in modern health care systems. However, they have more severe consequences in the presence of high and rising costs.

Surprisingly, relatively little is known about the factors which drive the rapid increase in expenditure.[5] An aging population, measured by the population share above a certain age threshold (e.g., 65 or 75 years) is sometimes considered as a possible explanation. However, as shown by Zweifel et al. (1999), patients' remaining life expectancy ("proximity to death") can better predict health care expenditure than does aging.[6]

In contrast, technological progress is widely believed to be a major cause for rising health care expenditure.[7] However, only few studies are concerned with evaluating its quantitative effect. Recently, Dormont et al. (2006) use microsimulation methods to identify the components of the upward drift in the expenditure of their sample population between 1992 and 2000. They find that changes in "medical practice" accounted for most of the increase. This measure captures changes in physicians' behavior or in patients' preferences as well as the impact of techno-

3 Ma and Mc Guire (1997) provide a formal analysis of the physician-patient relationship in a context of ex post moral hazard.

4 Source: OECD Health Data (2008).

5 See also Hartwig (2008).

6 In recent years, the hypothesis that aging does not play an important role for health care expenditure has found much support. Breyer, Lorenz and Niebel (2009) object that this question can be answered only when longitudinal data on the development of expenditure becomes available. They provide evidence that *both* the mortality rate and remaining life expectancy have an important effect.

7 See Newhouse (1992).

logical change. The authors conjecture that most of the compound effect can be attributed to technological progress, especially with regard to pharmaceutical expenditure. Moreover, the projected effect of medical practice was 3.8 times as large as that of aging.

It has also been mentioned that the process of adopting new, cost-intensive medical technologies is accelerated by moral hazard effects, a phenomenon referred to as dynamic moral hazard.[8] In this sense, asymmetric information may indeed contribute to the increase in expenditure.

A related explanation is the so-called cost disease described by Baumol (1967). According to this theory, productivity growth resulting from technological innovation only occurs in capital intensive industries. In contrast, service industries (e.g., health care or culture) are characterized by a constant labor productivity over time. Productivity growth in the capital intensive sector causes wages in both sectors to rise. This raises the relative price of services, such as health care. While Baumol's analysis is based on several simplifying assumptions, recent empirical evidence confirms his theory. Namely, Hartwig (2008) shows that wage increases in excess of productivity growth contributed significantly to the rise in health care expenditure in OECD countries.

If the cost disease is the main source of the increase in health care spending, not much can be done about it. The only remedy would be to raise productivity in the health care sector as well. This could be achieved, to some extent, by employing efficiency-enhancing technologies or by improving the organization of health care provision.[9]

The emergence of managed care can indeed be seen as a way to organize the supply of health care more efficiently. Managed care is now the predominant form of health insurance in the United States. For illustration, only 3% of the privately insured population were enrolled in traditional health insurance in 2007, whereas the majority chose one of different types of managed care plans.[10] Under managed care, the insurer acts as a contractual intermediary between consumers and health care providers (mainly hospitals and physician groups). The idea behind this is that the overconsumption of health care services may be addressed more effectively by

[8] See Baumgardner (1991), Selder (2005).

[9] See also Hartwig (2008).

[10] Source: Kaiser Family Foundation (2008).

providing appropriate incentives to physicians than through consumer copayments only.[11]

In practice, managed care organizations use a wide range of instruments to "manage" the supply of health care services. These especially involve prospective payment schemes to compensate physicians and hospitals. Additionally, consumers are often obliged to register with a primary care physician for a certain time period in advance. The physician also acts as a gatekeeper for specialist medical services. That is, specialist or hospital treatment cannot be obtained without the gatekeeper's permission. Moreover, patients have access only to physicians and hospitals that are part of the insurer's provider network, or they have to incur substantial copayments when visiting another provider.[12]

While managed care was initially confined to the private sector, elements of it have been introduced in several public health care systems as well. More generally, governments are increasingly relying on market forces as a way to limit health care spending. Several countries have enacted regulations to foster competition between insurers who offer the social health insurance package. In Germany, insurers may now contract individually with health care providers, which enables them to implement managed care arrangements. Managed care is also offered in the Netherlands, in Switzerland and in the public Medicare and Medicaid programs in the United States.

These innovations may also have downsides. First of all, managed care as such is suspected to reduce the quality of health care. In this context, most studies suggest that there are few consistent differences between the quality of treatment provided in managed care and traditional health insurance.[13] There is evidence, however, that poor and chronically ill patients receive a lower quality of treatment under managed care.[14]

Regulated competition between health insurers indeed creates incentives for risk selection.[15] In a social health insurance system, insurers are not allowed to charge premiums based on individual health risk. Consequently, they have an incentive to

[11] See Ellis and McGuire (1993).
[12] See Glied (2000) for a more detailed survey of managed care instruments.
[13] See Cutler et al. (2000), Polsky and Nicholson (2004).
[14] See Miller and Luft (1997) for a survey, and Duggan (2002) for more recent evidence.
[15] See Pauly (1984).

attract low-risk consumers and to reject high-risk individuals. To prevent risk selection (also referred to as cream skimming), insurers are required to enroll all applicants regardless of their risk type. In addition, many countries have introduced risk adjustment schemes to compensate insurers for differences in risk profiles. Therefore, insurers with a less favorable risk structure receive compensation payments from a common fund.

However, existing risk adjustment models predict individual health care costs only imperfectly and do not sufficiently reduce incentives for cream skimming. Insurers can still make substantial profits by selecting good risks, and they may indeed find ways to do so. For instance, most managed care instruments may be tools for selection as well. Numerous studies have shown that managed care organizations attract "healthier" individuals than those enrolled in traditional insurance.[16]

From a theoretical perspective, the problem of risk selection is closely related to another type of informational asymmetry in the health insurance market, concerning the consumer's (ex ante) risk type. Ever since the seminal contribution by Rothschild and Stiglitz (1976), competitive insurance markets are suspected to exhibit adverse selection.[17] If consumers are better informed on their individual risk type than is the insurer, a separating equilibrium will arise: high risks are fully insured at a fair premium, whereas low risks cannot obtain full coverage. Moreover, if the proportion of low risks is sufficiently small, an equilibrium will arise where only high risks are insured at all.

In a regulated insurance market, risk selection need not be based on asymmetric information between the consumer and the insurer. Instead, the incentive for cream skimming arises because insurers are not allowed to exploit their information on consumers' health risks, that is, to set actuarially fair premiums. Risk selection based on insurer information is also referred to as direct risk selection.

In the case of *indirect* selection, insurers try to induce self-selection among consumers. Managed care organizations, in particular, may offer services which are attractive to healthy individuals (such as preventive care), to an extent that is not justified from an efficiency perspective. On the other hand, treatment for chronic conditions may be rationed, for example, by avoiding to contract with specialists. In particular, an equilibrium of the Rothschild-Stiglitz type may be established.[18]

[16] See Cutler and Reber (1998), Frank et al. (2000).
[17] See also Zweifel (2005).

Against this background, it is crucial to know whether managed care can raise the productivity of the medical sector. Alternatively, the premium discount of managed care plans relative to traditional insurance might be due to risk selection. To avoid measuring selection effects, Cutler et al. (2000) focus on the effect of managed care on the treatment costs of heart attacks. They argue that patients suffering from this condition have similar characteristics, independent of their insurance status. The authors find that health maintenance organizations (HMOs) [19] had 30% to 40% lower expenditure than conventional insurers. However, this reduction was mainly due to the fact that HMOs paid the hospital a lower price for the same service, and not to increases in treatment efficiency.[20] This result has been confirmed in other studies.[21]

Finally, there is also evidence that managed care may raise productivity. Focusing on the Medicare sector, Acemoglu and Finkelstein (2008) show that the changeover towards prospective payment of hospitals in the 1980s lead to changes in the pattern of technology adoption. As a consequence, the capital-labor ratio increased substantially. The study suggests that the investment pattern has changed from quality-enhancing technologies more toward cost-saving technologies.

1.2 Outlook

The next two chapters are concerned with two particular problems related to managed care on the one hand, and cream skimming in a context of imperfect risk adjustment on the other hand.

Apart from the instruments mentioned above, managed care organizations control consumers' access to medical treatment by "utilization review". This involves the pre-authorization of hospitalizations and other costly treatments. Through the authorization process, the insurer (or a third party) may deny coverage for treat-

[18] See Glazer and McGuire (2000). Other studies of indirect risk selection involve Frank et al. (2000), Kifmann (2002), Biglaiser and Ma (2003), Jack (2006).

[19] An HMO is a type of managed care organization characterized by relatively strong restrictions of consumer choice and access to medical treatment. See Glied (2000).

[20] Managed care organizations have greater bargaining power than traditional insurers because they can bargain individually with providers, and can limit consumers' provider choice. See Gal-Or (1997,1999) for an analysis of related industrial organization aspects.

[21] See Polsky and Nicholson (2004).

ment prescribed by an insured's physician. Thus, the insurer assumes a gatekeeping function as well. In the United States, these measures have provoked much criticism: while patients complain about treatment denials, physicians fear that their professional authority is being undermined.

The next chapter presents a formal model of utilization review, based on a seminal paper on authority by Aghion and Tirole (1997). A main characteristic of utilization review is that the insurer can intervene in medical decision making after the health insurance contract and the physician payment contract have been signed. This may result in a commitment problem.

In the contractual equilibrium described in Chapter 2, utilization review has a negative effect on the physician's incentive to exert a diagnostic effort because the physician's information becomes less relevant for the treatment decision. Due to the sequential nature of the game, the insurer may not internalize this effect at the review stage. Thus, there may be too much monitoring in equilibrium. As a consequence, too many patients for whom treatment would be efficient are not referred by the physician at all. The model suggests that the criticism against managed care is partly justified. Nevertheless, utilization review represents a valuable instrument to control moral hazard if the commitment problem can be solved.

Chapter 3 is concerned with insurers' incentives to practice *direct* risk selection when there is imperfect risk adjustment. First, the effects of a statistical (or "conventional") risk adjustment scheme, which compensates for predictable differences in expected health care costs, are analyzed. In the model, both the regulator and the insurer can initially observe a signal (for example, consumers' age), on which the transfer payments may be conditioned. Alternatively, there may be no risk adjustment at all. An obvious advantage of risk adjustment is that it causes the insurer to accept consumers with "unfavorable" characteristics (here, elderly people), who would be unprofitable otherwise.

The insurer can still make profits by screening out consumers who are high risks relative to their cost group (or age group). Generally, the information which is necessary to do so may be costly to obtain. Given this assumption, it is shown that *imperfect* risk adjustment (based on an exogenous signal) may raise incentives for cream skimming. This is surprising, because it is often assumed that even a highly imperfect risk adjustment scheme is superior to a situation without risk adjustment.

In the second part of the analysis, an optimal payment scheme based on cost sharing between the regulator and the insurer is derived. It is shown that the optimal cost share incurred by the insurer is decreasing in expected (rather than realized) health care expenditure. Thus, the insurer's private information on consumers' risk types can be extracted. In practice, insurers could designate certain fractions of consumers for one or different risk pools involving partial cost reimbursement.

Apart from controlling overconsumption as such, managed care organizations often try to standardize medical decision making. By doing so, they can build up a reputation for promoting certain treatment standards. In general, medical decision making is more and more being based on standards and guidelines. The fourth chapter is concerned with the question of *how* medical decisions should be taken in a particular context. A dynamic decision situation is considered where a disease need not be treated immediately. Instead, the physician can delay the decision and observe how the patient's health state evolves over time. "Watchfully waiting" is considered a relevant treatment alternative for many types of diseases.

A key aspect of the physician's decision is exactly when to perform a medical intervention. Standard theory suggests that treatment should be provided if (when) the present value of its benefits exceeds the present value of its costs. This, however, ignores the possibility that new information about the patient's condition may be revealed over time. Waiting has an option value, while carrying out the medical intervention extinguishes the option and sacrifices its value. As a consequence, the net present value of treatment has to be (possibly substantially) greater than zero to trigger intervention. Chapter 4 contains a formal model of the watchfully waiting process. Optimal decision rules for switching to direct medical intervention are derived. The approach could be applied to a wide range of decision problems in health economics and medicine.

Finally, Chapter 5 contains some brief, concluding remarks. Technical proofs are relegated to the appendices at the end of each chapter.

Chapter 2

Managed Care and Physician Incentives: A Theory of Utilization Review

2.1 Introduction

"Utilization review" is employed by managed care organizations and other health insurers to monitor physicians' use of health care services. This especially involves the pre-authorization of hospitalizations and other costly treatments. Through the authorization process, the insurer (or a third party) may deny coverage for medical treatment prescribed by an insured's physician. In the United States, most managed care organizations, which cover the majority of the privately insured population, make use of utilization review.[1] For illustration, firms which are engaged by insurers to provide third party review oversee the supply of health care services for more than 100 million people.[2]

These measures are controversial and have provoked much criticism against managed care. Patients' fear of unjustified denials of treatment and physicians' complaints about challenges to their professional authority and autonomy resulted

---

1 To a lesser extent, utilization review is also used in several public health care systems in Europe. In Germany, for example, physicians have to ask for a second medical opinion when they prescribe certain expensive pharmaceuticals.

2 See Wolff and Schlesinger (1998).

in the so-called managed care backlash in the 1990s.[3] Since then, insurers have also started to question the value of utilization review. For example, United Health Care, one of the largest managed care organizations in the US, abandoned its utilization review program in 1999 in favor of a more consumer oriented approach.[4]

This paper argues that insurers should not intervene too much in medical decision making. Assuming that utilization review is an instrument to reduce overconsumption of health care services, it is shown that insurers tend to exert excessive effort for monitoring. Welfare losses may occur if the insurer cannot commit to a level of intervention at the contractual stage.

The results are derived in a framework of moral hazard: a primary care physician has to exert effort to make a diagnosis (hidden action), and to refer those individuals to specialist or hospital treatment for whom this is efficient (hidden information). Assuming that the physician is compensated by a simple cost-sharing contract, the second-best solution involves both over- and undertreatment. On the one hand, the physician refers some patients whose benefit of treatment falls below the cost. On the other hand, diagnosis effort is inefficiently low, implying that some patients for whom treatment would be efficient remain undiagnosed.

In the contractual equilibrium, utilization review has a negative effect on the physician's effort choice as it reduces the value of physician information. This effect, however, may not be internalized by the insurer at the review stage. In the absence of commitment, distortions arise even if the insurer maximizes social welfare and does not make "unjustified" denials. An extension of the model shows that the equilibrium can be improved upon when a more sophisticated payment scheme is used. Even the first-best solution may be reached with a contract conditional on the final treatment (approval) decision. However, it is questionable whether this solution can be implemented in practice. Instead, delegation of utilization review to a third party may be helpful to solve the insurer's commitment problem.

A main objective of the paper is to analyze how managed care instruments, in this case utilization review, can be used to supplement an incomplete physician payment contract. Many health economists have mentioned that it is hard to provide efficient financial incentives to a health care supplier who makes non-contractible choices along several dimensions (for example, cost efficiency, quality or appropri-

[3] See Luft (1999), Miller (2006).

[4] See Wickizer and Lessler (2002).

ateness of treatment).[5] Thus, there is scope for non-financial instruments to improve upon the contractual outcome. This incompleteness is reflected by the assumption that the benefit of treatment cannot be contracted upon.

The insight that a principal's (insurer) intervention can negatively affect an agent's (physician) incentives to exert effort is owed to Aghion and Tirole (1997). The authors develop a theory of authority based on an incomplete contracting approach, which is adapted here to a health economics framework. According to Aghion and Tirole, a managed care organization has the "formal" authority over the provision of health care. The insurer's intervention may be necessary because the insurance contract does not fully specify the conditions under which treatment is appropriate.

A few other authors have identified commitment problems as a source of quality distortions under managed care. In particular, Miller (2006) shows that vertical integration between an insurer and a group of physicians (a structure which represents managed care insurance) reduces the quality of treatment, compared with the case of non-integration (corresponding to "traditional" health insurance). The integrated firm lacks credibility to provide more than a minimum level of quality because it cannot use physician incentive contracts as a commitment device.

Independently from this paper, Arlen an MacLeod (2005) make an argument similar to the one presented here. However, the authors rely on stronger assumptions regarding the insurer's commitment problem. In particular, they assume that the insurer can deny coverage in the review process even if treatment is efficient. In contrast, this case is ruled out in the present paper. Focusing on the effect of liability rules on the treatment decision, Arlen and MacLeod argue that managed care organizations should be held liable for negligent acts committed by their physicians.

The paper is also related to the literature on general practice and gatekeeping.[6] In a gatekeeping system, patients who seek specialist treatment need to obtain the permission of a primary care physician (gatekeeper) first. Malcomson (2004) shows that a gatekeeper who is responsible for the cost of specialist treatment may have too much an incentive to acquire information on the cost. As a result, fewer patients will be referred than it would be efficient. In contrast, the present paper is concerned with a situation where both the physician and the insurer act as gatekeepers.

[5] See Ma (1994), Chalkley and Malcomson (1998), Malcomson (2004), Eggleston (2005).

[6] See also Jelovac (2001), Garcia Mariñoso and Jelovac (2003), Brekke et al. (2007).

Dranove and Spier (2003) provide an alternative interpretation of utilization review. They assume that both the physician and the insurer (or review agency) have some private information on the patient's benefit from treatment. If the physician payment contract involves inefficient decision-making, a welfare-maximizing review agency will improve the situation. Interestingly, a more restrictive approval threshold may induce the physician to recommend treatment more often.

Newhouse and Lindsey (1988) argue that second opinion programs - which constitute a form of utilization review - may worsen health outcomes in the presence of diagnostic errors. If only those patients who are recommended for hospital treatment seek a second opinion, the number of patients who are wrongly rejected by the second physician may be higher than the number of correctly denied cases.

There is mixed evidence on the effects of utilization review on cost efficiency and quality of treatment. Among other studies, Cutler et al. (2000) and Polsky and Nicholson (2004) find little difference in the actual utilization of health care services between managed care and traditional health insurance. In contrast, studies on particular utilization review programs suggest that these may be quite effective at reducing the use of hospital services.[7] Wickizer and Lessler (2002) argue that there is little evidence on the effects of utilization review on total health care costs. The reduction in hospital days might be (partly) offset by increases in the use of primary care services.

The remainder of the paper is organized as follows. The model is presented in the next section. Section 2.3 analyzes the optimal cost-sharing contract between the physician and the insurer in the absence of utilization review. Section 2.4 is concerned with the effect of utilization review on physician incentives and with the insurer's commitment problem. In Section 2.5, several extensions of the basic model are discussed. Finally, Section 2.6 concludes.

2.2 The Model

We analyze the relationship between a patient, a physician and an insurer in a managed care framework. The patient purchases health insurance coverage from the insurer, who contracts with the physician on the provision of medical care. Im-

[7] See, for example, Rosenberg et al. (1995).

plicitly, there is also a provider of specialist care in the model (the hospital) who, however, does not play an active role.

The Patient and the Insurance Contract. All individuals are identical in their health risk ex ante. The utility function is assumed to be separable in health and money, such that the optimal treatment decision becomes independent of wealth. After the insurance contract is signed, the representative patient suffers from a particular disease, which occurs with probability one, but varies by its severity. This is captured by the random variable b, distributed with density $f(b)$ and cumulative distribution function $F(b)$ on the interval $[\underline{b}, \bar{b}]$. The variable b represents the patient's benefit from hospital treatment, net of any disutility. The cost of treatment, denoted by c, is constant, with $0 \leq \underline{b} < c < \bar{b}$. Moreover, the inverse hazard rate $[1 - F(b)]/f(b)$ is (weakly) increasing.[8]

The patient is unaware of b and seeks diagnosis. He is restricted by the insurance contract to visit the primary care physician first, who may refer him to the hospital for treatment. For simplicity, we assume that the physician cannot provide treatment himself. The patient does not incur any copayments for the services of the physician or the hospital. Being fully insured, he would always like to receive treatment, even if the cost exceeds the benefit. The managed care arrangement provides a way to control this ex post moral hazard. As it is not our aim to compare different types of health insurance, this is taken as exogenous. We also assume the patient to be risk neutral, thus focusing on the insurer's regulatory function.

The Physician and the Treatment Decision. To model the physician-patient relationship, we assume that the physician maximizes a weighted sum of the patient's benefit and his own profit. This may be attributed to the physician's altruism or to professional ethics. Many health economists consider these factors as an important determinant of physician behavior, apart from pure profit maximization.[9] If treatment is provided, the physician derives a direct utility θb, with $\theta \in (0,1)$. Thus he does not fully internalize the patient's benefit. Alternatively, the parameter θ may be interpreted to reflect the effect of the treatment outcome on the physician's reputation.

[8] This is only a sufficient condition for the insurer's problem to be concave.

[9] See Ellis and McGuire (1986), Chalkley and Malcomson (1998), Jack (2005).

The physician needs to exert effort to make a diagnosis. Following Aghion and Tirole (1997), we assume that he learns the correct benefit of treatment with probability e. With probability $1-e$, he remains uninformed and can only observe the benefit distribution. The effort cost function $g(e)$ is strictly increasing and convex, and satisfies $g(0)=0$, $g'(0)=0$ and $g'(1)=\infty$. Moreover, we assume that $g'''(e)\geq 0$. It is convenient to rule out the possibility of an incorrect diagnosis.

The physician's effort is unobservable to the insurer. Although in practice, some aspects of a diagnosis (for example, a blood test or an X-ray) may be verifiable, it is hard to determine how much time and consideration the physician has invested to learn the patient's condition. Moreover, b is considered as "soft" information, implying that it cannot be costlessly verified by the insurer. In the present context, the physician's decision rule can be defined by a threshold value $\hat{b}$, such that a patient of type $[\hat{b},\bar{b}]$ is referred to the hospital, whereas the other types remain untreated. Thus, in case of a referral, the insurer can only infer that $b\geq\hat{b}$.

Utilization review is modeled as follows. If the physician makes a referral, the insurer can also exert a non-contractible effort to learn the benefit from treatment. The insurer becomes fully informed with probability a, and the effort cost function $h(a)$ satisfies the standard properties. After acquiring information, the insurer decides whether to approve treatment. For reasons discussed below, the insurer does not deny treatment when its benefit exceeds the cost.

The Contractual Environment. At the ex ante stage, the insurer proposes a contract to the physician who offers his services in a competitive market. The physician is bound to a participation constraint, and the reservation utility is normalized to zero. The contract specifies a capitation t, which is paid to the physician in advance, and a copayment m, incurred by the physician if treatment is provided. This corresponds to a standard cost-sharing contract, including the special cases of purely prospective payment $(m=c)$ and full cost reimbursement $(m=0)$. Accordingly, this specification captures most payment schemes which are commonly used to compensate health care providers. In contrast, we assume that it is too costly to write a contract conditional on b. This can be justified because the treatment technology may change over time, or because the individual benefit from treatment may be hard to describe in general.

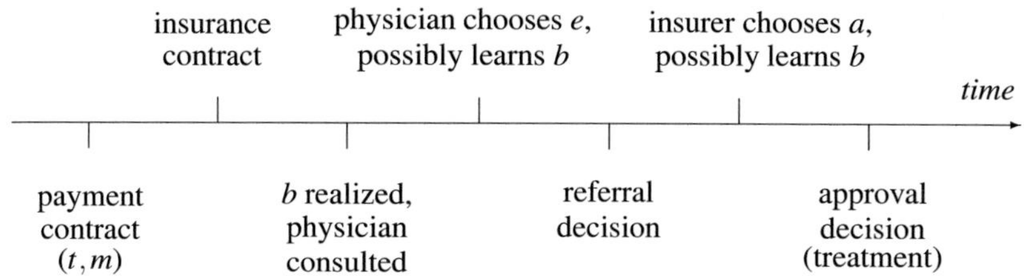

Figure 2.1: Time structure.

Although the physician is willing to forgo some profits (since $\theta > 0$), it seems appropriate to assume that he does not accept a loss-making contract ex ante. Therefore, the participation constraint takes the form

$$t - q \cdot m - g(e) \geq 0$$

where q denotes the probability of treatment. This assumption prevents that the insurer attaches excessive weight $(1 + \theta)$ to the patient's benefit.[10]

The insurer operates in a perfectly competitive market. Health insurance is offered at a fair premium, denoted by p. The patient can observe the contract (t,m) and anticipates its effects on the treatment decision. Consequently, the insurer maximizes consumer welfare, subject to the physician's participation constraint and the break-even condition:

$$p = t + q(c - m) + r \cdot h(a)$$

Here, r represents the probability of utilization review, which is equal to the probability of a referral. The choices of a, e and $\hat{b}$ are discussed in the following section.

Compared to the related literature on managed care, the model is based on weaker assumptions regarding the insurer's commitment problem. Miller (2006) assumes that the insurer cannot commit to the physician payment contract, while Arlen and MacLeod (2005) suppose that treatment may be denied even if $b \geq c$. To summarize, Figure 2.1 illustrates the timing of the game.

[10] See Choné and Ma (2009) for a similar assumption.

2.3 The Case without Utilization Review

In this section, we consider a simplified version of the model where treatment decisions are not reviewed. The aim is to clarify the basic trade-off between diagnosis effort and treatment efficiency.

2.3.1 The Physician Agency Problem

As usual, the model is solved by backward induction, starting with the physician's referral decision. Once the physician has learned the patient's condition, he makes a referral if his own utility exceeds the copayment.

Lemma 1 *When informed, the physician refers the patient if $b > m/\theta$.*

In the following, we restrict the analysis to an equilibrium where the physician does not recommend treatment when uninformed.

Assumption 1 (informed referral) *In the model without utilization review, the optimal copayment satisfies $m > \theta E(b)$.*

In order to prevent a "blind" referral, the copayment must exceed the physician's expected utility attached to treatment. As discussed later, this imposes an implicit restriction on the model parameters. Assumption 1 seems realistic insofar as managed care organizations often provide physicians with strong financial incentives to save costs. Moreover, it rules out the unlikely situation that the insurer obtains more information on the patient's condition than does the physician.[11]

Clearly, by setting $m = \theta c$, the insurer could induce the physician to recommend treatment whenever it is efficient. However, efficiency at the referral stage must be traded off against the physician's incentive for information acquisition. The first-order condition for the choice of diagnostic effort is given by:

$$\int_{m/\theta}^{\bar{b}} (\theta b - m) dF(b) = g'(e) \tag{2.1}$$

[11] In practice, a "blind" referral may be attractive if the cost of hospital treatment is reimbursed by the insurer, whereas the physician is responsible for his own treatment costs. This does not seem very realistic in the context of managed care, where physicians are often under considerable pressure to save costs.

The left-hand side represents the marginal benefit derived by the physician from a raise in the probability of treatment. Implicit differentiation yields:

$$\frac{\partial e}{\partial m} = -\frac{1-F(\frac{m}{\theta})}{g''(e)} < 0 \tag{2.2}$$

$$\frac{\partial e}{\partial \theta} = \frac{1}{g''(e)} \int_{m/\theta}^{\bar{b}} b\, dF(b) > 0 \tag{2.3}$$

A reduction in m makes diagnostic information more valuable to the physician because the cost of an inframarginal referral (where $b > m/\theta$) is reduced. Moreover, taking the copayment as given, a more altruistic physician is willing to exert more effort as his benefit from a referral is relatively high.

Now, suppose that the insurer implements the efficient referral decision (that is, $m = \theta c$). The left-hand side of equation (2.1) can be written as:

$$\theta\,[1-F(c)]\,[E(b|\,b \geq c) - c]$$

Apart from the factor θ, this expression reflects the marginal *social* benefit from an increase in diagnostic effort, which is equal to the probability that treatment is efficient times the conditional expected net surplus. Since the physician is not a perfect agent ($\theta < 1$), diagnosis effort remains inefficiently low. The following analysis shows that it is optimal to allow some inefficient referrals in order to give the physician better incentives.

2.3.2 The Contractual Stage

Since both the insurance market and the market for physician services are competitive, the insurer's objective is to maximize social welfare, that is, the patient's expected utility minus treatment and diagnosis costs, subject to the incentive constraint (2.1):

$$\max_{e,m} L = e \int_{m/\theta}^{\bar{b}} (b-c)\, dF(b) - g(e) + \lambda \left(\int_{m/\theta}^{\bar{b}} (\theta b - m)\, dF(b) - g'(e) \right) \tag{2.4}$$

This expression is obtained after inserting the physician's participation constraint into the objective function. As the physician's maximization problem is strictly concave, the first-order approach can be applied without further restrictions. The first-order conditions of problem (2.4) are given by:

$$\frac{\partial L}{\partial e} = \int_{m/\theta}^{\bar{b}} (b-c)dF(b) - g'(e) - \lambda g''(e) = 0 \tag{2.5}$$

$$\frac{\partial L}{\partial m} = e\left(c - \frac{m}{\theta}\right) f\left(\frac{m}{\theta}\right)\frac{1}{\theta} - \lambda\left(1 - F\left(\frac{m}{\theta}\right)\right) = 0 \tag{2.6}$$

Combining equations (2.1), (2.5) and (2.6) yields:

$$\underbrace{f\left(\frac{m}{\theta}\right)\frac{e}{\theta}\left(c - \frac{m}{\theta}\right)}_{\frac{\partial W}{\partial m}(+)} + \underbrace{\int_{m/\theta}^{\bar{b}} [(1-\theta)b - (c-m)]dF(b)}_{\frac{\partial W}{\partial e}(+)}\underbrace{\left(-\frac{1-F(\frac{m}{\theta})}{g''(e)}\right)}_{\frac{\partial e}{\partial m}(-)} = 0 \tag{2.7}$$

Equation (2.7) shows the total effect of a change in the copayment on social welfare, denoted by W. At $m = \theta c$, the direct effect ($\partial W/\partial m$) becomes zero, and the whole expression is negative. This reflects the fact that too many patients for whom treatment would be efficient remain undiagnosed ($\partial W/\partial e > 0$). Under the above assumptions, the insurer's maximization problem is concave.[12] Thus, the copayment must be reduced.

Proposition 1 *In the second-best equilibrium, and given that Assumption 1 holds, the physician exerts an inefficiently low effort for diagnosis and refers too many patients when informed. The optimal copayment fulfills* $m^* < \theta c$.

The trade-off is illustrated in Figure 2.2. The horizontally and vertically striped triangles (weighted by the density of b) represent the social surplus and physician surplus from treatment, respectively. In the benchmark case ($m = \theta c$), the second area would become too small, reflecting that diagnosis effort would be lower than in the second-best equilibrium. Moreover, the triangle below the b-axis represents the welfare loss due to inefficient treatment.

Clearly, these distortions arise because the physician's objectives are not fully aligned with patient preferences, that is, $\theta < 1$. If the physician is relatively altru-

[12] The proofs of Proposition 1 and Remark 1 are in the Appendix.

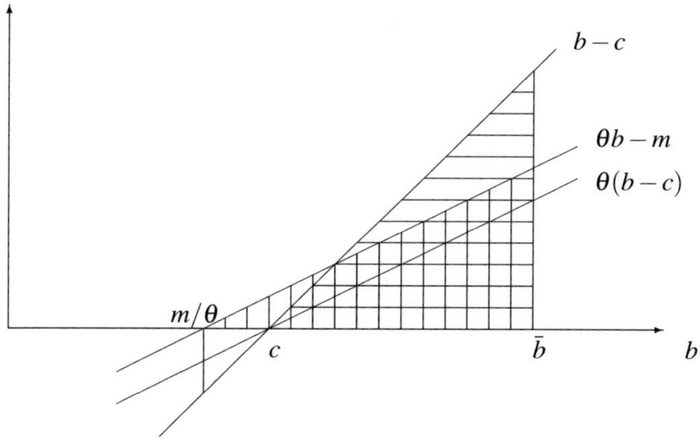

Figure 2.2: Social surplus and physician surplus from a referral.

istic (or if he is disciplined by an effective reputation mechanism), the welfare loss will be relatively small. In contrast, the effect of the agency parameter on the optimal copayment may be ambiguous. If θ is small, the copayment must be reduced far below the first-best value to induce a certain effort level. This, however, results in a relatively high proportion of inefficient referrals. It can be shown that the first effect dominates the second one if the level of physician altruism is relatively high. Remark 1 gives a sufficient condition.

Remark 1 *In the second-best equilibrium, social welfare is increasing in θ. Whenever $\theta \geq 1/2$, the copayment and the threshold benefit level for a referral (m/θ) are also increasing in this parameter.*

So far, it has been taken for granted that the physician makes an informed referral decision. An example is helpful to illustrate the role of Assumption 1 and to derive explicit results.

Example. Let b be uniformly distributed on the interval $[0,1]$ and consider the quadratic effort cost function $g(e) = e^2/2$. From the physician's first-order condition (2.1), we obtain the effort level $e = (\theta/2)\left(1 - \frac{m}{\theta}\right)^2$. Inserting this into equation (2.7) and solving for m yields:

$$m^* = \frac{\theta}{2+\theta}\,[3c - 1 + \theta]$$

Here, the referral threshold is always increasing in θ:

$$\frac{d(m^*/\theta)}{d\theta} = -\frac{3c-1+\theta}{(2+\theta)^2} + \frac{\theta}{2+\theta} = \frac{3-3c}{(2+\theta)^2} > 0$$

Moreover, it can be shown that Assumption 1 reduces to $c > 2/3 - \theta/6$. That is, the treatment cost must exceed a minimum value between $1/2$ and $2/3$, depending on θ. This seems realistic insofar as utilization review is mostly applied for expensive treatments.

2.4 The General Case

In the second-best equilibrium, the insurer clearly has an incentive to review the physician's referral decisions. The effects of this strategy are analyzed in the following. Here, utilization review is considered as a purely corrective instrument. That is, the insurer may overrule the physician's decision, but does not impose any financial sanctions in this case.

2.4.1 Utilization Review

Although the insurer maximizes social welfare ex ante, this may not be true at the review stage. The disciplining effect of the market cannot be taken as given any more. As firm behavior generally depends on the institutional environment, the objective function is not clear. We consider two possibilities:

Case 1. As a benchmark case, assume that the insurer maximizes the social surplus resulting from the approval decision. Due to the sequential nature of the game, however, the number of referrals is taken as given at this stage.

Case 2. Suppose that the physician can appeal a treatment denial. There is an external reviewer (appeal agency) who can perfectly observe the benefit of treatment and maximizes social welfare. Therefore, a denial is overturned if $b \geq c$.[13] Notice that the physician has indeed an incentive to appeal an unjustified denial: a sufficient condition here is that any transaction cost does not exceed the value $\theta c - m$. In equilibrium, the insurer approves treatment when it is efficient, and there is no appeal. Moreover, we assume that the insurer is only concerned with his own profit at this stage, but not with the patient's benefit. In this sense, the two cases represent two opposite extremes.[14]

Analogously to Assumption 1 ruling out a blind referral, the possibility of an uninformed denial is also excluded.

Assumption 2 (informed denial) *The insurer always approves treatment when uninformed.*

Under welfare maximization (Case 1), Assumption 2 holds if $E(b|\, b \geq \frac{m}{\theta}) \geq c$, i.e., if treatment is efficient for the average patient referred by the physician. Notice that in the model *without* utilization review, this is equivalent to $\partial W / \partial e \geq 0$. We can conclude that the assumption still holds if the equilibrium value of a is not too high.

In Case 2, it must be further assumed that the insurer incurs a cost (in the form of a fine or a loss in reputation) when a denial is overturned by the appeal agency.[15] Otherwise, the insurer would always deny treatment, and would not acquire any information. To rule out this strategy, the punishment must be at least equal to $(c-m)[F(c) - F(\frac{m}{\theta})]/[1 - F(\frac{m}{\theta})]$. Clearly, this value corresponds to the expected cost savings from avoiding inefficient treatment.

[13] This is of course a simplifying assumption. Notice that several US states have introduced mandatory external review of treatment denials.

[14] Of course, we could also assume that the insurer partly internalizes the patient's utility, for example, due to a concern for reputation.

[15] See Malcomson (2004) for a similar assumption.

Information Acquisition. In Case 1, the insurer's objective function is given by the following expression:

$$\max_a \; a\int_{m/\theta}^{c}(c-b)\,dF(b\,|\,b\geq m/\theta)-h(a)$$

The first-order condition for the choice of monitoring effort can be written as:

$$\frac{1}{1-F(m/\theta)}\int_{m/\theta}^{c}(c-b)\,dF(b)=h'(a) \tag{2.8}$$

In contrast, in Case 2, the insurer does not take into account the foregone patient benefit, but only his own cost savings resulting from a denial. Thus, the first-order condition takes the form:

$$\frac{F(c)-F(m/\theta)}{1-F(m/\theta)}\,(c-m)=h'(a) \tag{2.9}$$

In both cases, the insurer's level of information is independent of the physician's effort. This is due to the timing of the game, and to the fact that utilization review occurs only when the patient has been diagnosed. Moreover, it can be easily shown that a is decreasing in the physician's copayment. This is intuitive because stronger financial incentives can be seen as a substitute for utilization review. In Case 2, there is also a direct negative effect since the insurer's cost share is decreasing in m. Finally, an increase in the agency parameter θ raises the insurer's incentive for monitoring, ceteris paribus.

2.4.2 The Physician's Decision

Turning to the physician's decision, the assumption ruling out the possibility of a blind referral must be restated.

Assumption 3 (informed referral) *In the equilibrium with utilization review, the optimal copayment satisfies:*

$$(1-a)\,[\theta E(b)-m^*]+a\,[1-F(c)]\,[\theta E(b|\,b\geq c)-m^*]<0$$

The left-hand side represents the physician's expected utility from an uninformed referral. Clearly, the first part pertains to the case where the insurer is also uninformed, whereas the second part corresponds to the situation where the insurer has learned b.

At the diagnosis stage, the physician's effort choice is characterized by the following first-order condition:

$$\int_{m/\theta}^{\bar{b}} (\theta b - m)\, dF(b) - a \int_{m/\theta}^{c} (\theta b - m)\, dF(b) = g'(e) \tag{2.10}$$

Differentiation yields:

$$\frac{\partial e}{\partial a} = -\frac{1}{g''(e)} \int_{m/\theta}^{c} (\theta b - m)\, dF(b) < 0 \tag{2.11}$$

$$\frac{\partial e}{\partial m} = \frac{-[1 - F(m/\theta)] + a[F(c) - F(m/\theta)]}{g''(e)} < 0 \tag{2.12}$$

Intuitively, utilization review has a negative effect on physician incentives. With increasing monitoring effort, the patient becomes more likely to be rejected, and the physician's information becomes less relevant for the treatment decision. As before, the physician's effort is decreasing in the copayment m and can be shown to be increasing in the agency parameter θ.

2.4.3 Contracting and the Commitment Problem

The main problem with utilization review is that the insurer does not internalize the effect of his effort choice on physician incentives. To formally analyze the commitment problem, it is convenient to compare the sequential game to a situation where the insurer can commit to a monitoring effort ex ante.

Consider the insurer's optimization problem at the contractual stage. In the case without commitment, this amounts to maximizing

$$W = e\left(\int_{m/\theta}^{\bar{b}} (b - c)\, dF(b) + a \int_{m/\theta}^{c} (c - b)\, dF(b) - \left[1 - F\left(\frac{m}{\theta}\right)\right] h(a) \right) - g(e)$$

subject to the first-order conditions for the physician's and insurer's effort choices. In Case 1, where the ability to commit is less restricted, the Lagrangian takes the form:

$$\max_{e,\,a,\,m} \; L = W + \lambda \left(\int_{m/\theta}^{\bar{b}} (\theta b - m)\, dF(b) - a \int_{m/\theta}^{c} (\theta b - m)\, dF(b) - g'(e) \right)$$
$$+ \mu \left(\frac{1}{1 - F(m/\theta)} \int_{m/\theta}^{c} (c - b)\, dF(b) - h'(a) \right)$$

Accordingly, in Case 2, the last line is to be replaced using equation (2.9).

While it is hard to determine whether the contractual problem is well-behaved, we can draw some conclusions regarding its general properties. The first-order condition for the choice of m takes the following form:

$$\frac{\partial W}{\partial m} + \frac{\partial W}{\partial e}\frac{\partial e}{\partial m} + \underbrace{\left(\frac{\partial W}{\partial a} + \frac{\partial W}{\partial e}\frac{\partial e}{\partial a} \right)}_{\frac{dW}{da}\,(-)} \frac{\partial a}{\partial m} = 0$$

Since the insurer can anticipate the level of utilization review, the copayment is adjusted in order to reduce the welfare losses caused by excessive monitoring. Notice that in Case 1, the insurer's marginal effort cost equals the direct welfare gain from utilization review (such that $\partial W/\partial a = 0$). Therefore, the distortion is due to the externality on physician effort only. In contrast, in Case 2, there is an additional welfare loss because the insurer's objective function at the review stage is not aligned with social preferences ($\partial W/\partial a < 0$). This is referred to as the agency effect.

In the case *with* commitment, the insurer makes an unconstrained effort choice, such that $\mu = 0$. The first-order conditions can be written in a stylized form as:

$$\frac{dW}{dm} = \frac{\partial W}{\partial m} + \frac{\partial W}{\partial e}\frac{\partial e}{\partial m} = 0; \qquad \frac{dW}{da} = \frac{\partial W}{\partial a} + \frac{\partial W}{\partial e}\frac{\partial e}{\partial a} = 0$$

The second derivatives d^2W/dm^2 and d^2W/da^2 are negative. Therefore, it is still optimal to allow some inefficient referrals ($m < \theta c$). Moreover, the second equation implies that the insurer wants to restrain himself from excessive monitoring.

Proposition 2 *At the contractual stage, the insurer would like to choose a lower effort for utilization review, compared to the sequential equilibrium.*[16]

Notice that this result can be derived from the fact that $\partial W/\partial a > 0$, and does not rely on the assumption that the problem for the sequential case must be concave.

For illustration, suppose that the insurer cannot directly commit to a, but can write an incentive contract for an external reviewer, which reduces the payoff from utilization review to a proportion α of the initial value. The first-order condition (2.9) changes to:

$$\frac{F(c)-F(m/\theta)}{1-F(m/\theta)}\,\alpha\,(c-m)=h'(a)$$

According to the above result and discussion, we must have $\alpha < 1$ in order to maximize social welfare.

Clearly, Proposition 2 is valid for both cases regarding the insurer's commitment problem. Since the level of monitoring is higher in Case 2 than in Case 1, the following statement applies.

Remark 2 *If the insurer cannot commit to an effort choice, the resulting welfare loss is greater in Case 2 than in Case 1.*

How does the contractual trade-off compare to that of the model without utilization review? On the one hand, a reduction in the physician's copayment below θc causes less distortion because some inefficient referrals can be avoided. On the other hand, a reduction in m further aggravates the insurer's commitment problem as the incentive for monitoring increases.

In the example shown below, the optimal copayment is lower in Case 1 than in the reference case without utilization review, implying a more generous referral behavior. In Case 2, in contrast, m is raised above the reference level to limit the welfare loss caused by the agency effect.

Example. The table shows the results for the example with a uniformly distributed treatment benefit, and $\theta = c = 2/3$. The effort cost functions are quadratic: $g(e) = 0.1\,e^2$ and $h(a) = 0.045\,a^2$.[17]

[16] Proof: See the Appendix.
[17] We denote $W' = W \cdot 1000$.

No Utilization Review	No Commitment (Case 2)	No Commitment (Case 1)	Commitment	First Best
$W' = 14.6484$	$W' = 14.1098$	$W' = 14.6569$	$W' = 14.6570$	$W' = 15.4321$
$m = 0.41\overline{6}$	$m = 0.4322$	$m = 0.4162$	$m = 0.4162$	$\theta c = 0.\overline{4}$
$e = 0.4687$	$e = 0.4119$	$e = 0.4703$	$e = 0.4704$	$e = 0.\overline{5}$
	$a = 0.2713$	$a = 0.0532$	$a = 0.0475$	

Table 2.1: Results for the example with a uniform distribution.

The welfare loss due to the externality effect (Case 1) is quite small, which is of course related to the choice of the model parameters. Moreover, welfare is still higher than in the case without utilization review. This does not apply in the second case: here, utilization review has a negative effect on social welfare. It can also be verified that the conditions of Assumptions 2 and 3 are fulfilled.

In conclusion, it should be emphasized that utilization review can be a valuable tool to reduce moral hazard, despite possible distortions. In the course of time, insurers will probably find ways to mitigate the commitment problem. For example, utilization review may be delegated to a third party with weaker incentives for monitoring.

The above results have been derived under simplifying assumptions regarding the physician payment contract. Arguably, utilization review can still be a useful instrument in more general situations. In the present model, even the first-best solution can (theoretically) be implemented if the insurer's approval decision is contractible. These issues are discussed in the following section.

2.5 Extensions

On the one hand, a higher welfare level may be achieved through a more complete payment contract, or through delegation of utilization review. On the other hand, there may also be further agency problems on the insurer's side, such as collusion between managed care organizations or risk selection.

2.5.1 Generalized Payment Contract

Although the benefit of treatment is not contractible, the insurer can improve upon the cost-sharing contract by including a payment contingent on the approval decision. In particular, the physician could be obliged to pay a penalty if an inefficient referral is detected and if treatment is thus denied. Since the coverage decision itself is verifiable, such a contract may generally be enforced. This incentive scheme is similar to the class of auditing problems, which have been extensively analyzed.[18] In the following, the basic properties of this scheme are discussed.

The incentive contract now specifies a transfer t, which is adapted to match the physician's participation constraint, a copayment m and a penalty x. For simplicity, the insurer is assumed to maximize social welfare at the review stage (Case 1). Suppose that the marginal patient for whom the physician is indifferent between a referral and no treatment is characterized by $b < c$. When referring the patient, the physician incurs the penalty with probability a and receives utility $\theta b - m$ otherwise. The following Lemma applies.

Lemma 2 *If the physician payment contract is contingent on the insurer's approval decision, the patient is referred whenever:*

$$b \geq \hat{b} = \min\left\{\frac{m}{\theta} + \frac{a}{1-a}\frac{x}{\theta}; c\right\}$$

Clearly, an increase in the penalty or in monitoring effort makes an inefficient referral less attractive. Since there is now an additional instrument to provide incentives to the physician, the trade-off between treatment efficiency and diagnosis effort is mitigated. The physician's first-order condition is given by:

$$\int_{\hat{b}}^{\bar{b}} (\theta b - m)\, dF(b) - a \int_{\hat{b}}^{c} (\theta b - m + x)\, dF(b) = g'(e) \qquad (2.13)$$

Starting from the equilibrium (with or without commitment) where $x = 0$, suppose that the penalty is raised by $(1-a)/a$ marginal units, whereas the copayment is reduced by one marginal unit. Thus, the threshold benefit level for a referral remains unchanged. Notice that the insurer's effort choice is also unaffected. In contrast, the

[18] See Baron and Besanko (1984), Nalebuff and Scharfstein (1987), Khalil (1997).

change in diagnostic effort is given by the following expression:

$$\frac{1}{g''(e)}\left(-(1-a)\left[F(c)-F(\hat{b})\right]+\left[1-F(\hat{b})\right]-a\left[F(c)-F(\hat{b})\right]\right)>0 \qquad (2.14)$$

The first summand is related to the change in x, whereas the other two terms correspond to the effect of reducing m on physician effort. Intuitively, the negative effect of an increase in the penalty, which only applies to a fraction $F(c)-F(\hat{b})$ of all patient types, is more than offset by the reduction in the copayment, applying to all referrals. Since the physician's effort is initially too low, the considered measure must have a positive effect on social welfare.

Proposition 3 *Social welfare can be raised by imposing a penalty on the physician in case of an inefficient referral.*

As before, the properties of the equilibrium depend on whether the insurer can commit to an effort level. Under full commitment, the effort choice need not be ex post optimal. Here, Remark 3 implies that efficient physician behavior can be induced (in principle) for any given probability a.

Remark 3 *Given that Assumption 1 holds, the insurer can implement the efficient diagnosis effort and referral decision with the following contract:*

$$x=\frac{1-a}{a}(\theta c-m); \qquad m=c-(1-\theta)E(b|\,b\geq c)$$

It is well known that the first-best solution can be approximated if the physician has unlimited liability.[19] For this purpose, the insurer imposes an arbitrarily high penalty ($x\to\infty$) and becomes informed with a very small probability ($a\to 0$). This prevents the physician from making an inefficient referral decision. Then, the copayment can be chosen such as to implement the optimal effort level.[20] Notice that this result also applies in the case without commitment. Here, the insurer's effort choice must be consistent with the physician's referral strategy. As the first-best

[19] See Nalebuff and Scharfstein (1987).

[20] A problem here is that the optimal copayment is relatively small, such that Assumption 1 may not hold anymore. For example, in the case with a uniformly distributed treatment benefit, we must have $c>1/(1+\theta)$, which is a stronger condition than before.

solution is approximated, the incentive for monitoring indeed goes to zero. Since $h'(0) = 0$, the insurer is just indifferent whether to become informed with a very small probability or whether to exert no effort. In equilibrium, the first option must be chosen.[21]

Although physicians (or physician groups) are often responsible for a substantial amount of treatment costs, the assumption of unlimited liability seems to be rather unrealistic. Moreover, maximum punishment may not be optimal if the physician is risk averse and if he may be erroneously punished. If the penalty is limited, increases in efficiency must be traded off against higher monitoring costs. As a result, treatment efficiency and diagnosis effort will still be distorted. It can be predicted that social welfare will be lower in the case without commitment than in the reference case, due to the additional constraint on the insurer's effort choice. Nevertheless, the possibility to contract upon the approval decision does make a difference.

Comment. In practice, managed care organizations do not apply contractual punishments when treatment is denied. This may seem surprising against the theoretical background. However, physicians may instead face an implicit threat that the insurer will not continue the relationship if specialist treatment is prescribed too often. This would have similar consequences as an explicit penalty. Arguably, a contractual punishment would not be easily accepted by many physicians in practice. Moreover, if the insurer can collect a penalty when denying treatment, there is an incentive to make too many denials. It is unclear whether this can be prevented by external regulation.

Another problem lies in the law regarding medical malpractice. In the United States, managed care organizations are not liable for damages or complications caused by insufficient treatment to the same extent as physicians are. Instead, an insurer's denial of treatment is regarded as a decision of coverage only. Ambiguous decisions are considered to arise from an incomplete health insurance contract, which does not fully specify the types of treatment to be covered. In contrast, physicians' decisions are judged on medical necessity and appropriateness. A physician who does not recommend treatment, or even who does not appeal a denial, is there-

[21] See Bolton (1987) for a similar argument.

fore more likely to be held liable than is an insurer who denies coverage. This may further aggravate both the physician's and the insurer's agency problem.[22]

2.5.2 Delegation as Commitment

Managed care organizations often delegate utilization review - and the authority to deny treatment - to third party firms. This has an obvious reason: most insurers do not have the capacity and medical personnel to monitor physicians' treatment decisions. However, delegation may also be used as a commitment device. As mentioned in Section 2.4, the commitment solution can be achieved by delegating utilization review to a third party who benefits less from monitoring than the insurer would do. A simple linear reward structure is sufficient to align the incentives of the external reviewer with the insurer's ex ante preferences.

Contracting with a third party as a commitment device has been extensively analyzed in the literature on monitoring and auditing. In general, the optimal policy may involve a higher or lower level of monitoring than the principal would choose in the absence of commitment.[23] To implement the commitment solution, the contract between the principal and the third party must be observable and non-renegotiable. Delegation has been shown to be optimal even if there are additional agency problems between the principal and the supervisor.[24]

As mentioned, some managed care organizations have relaxed their utilization review requirements, and there is a general trend towards insurance plans allowing more consumer choice. This can be interpreted as a market reaction to the commitment problem. Moreover, a study by Schlesinger et al. (1997) suggests that utilization review is often delegated to firms which deny only relatively few requests for treatment. The authors analyze a survey conducted among over 100 utilization review firms and find that these differ considerably in their review styles. However, the average rate of final denials was relatively low (about 6.5%), and many firms had even lower denial rates of about 1-2%.

[22] Arlen and MacLeod (2005) provide a formal analysis of these issues, and Danzon (1997) discusses several controversial cases.

[23] See, for example, Sappington (1986), Melumad and Mookherjee (1989).

[24] See Strausz (1997).

A problem that deserves further attention is that the delegation of utilization review may facilitate collusion between managed care organizations. To illustrate this possibility, suppose that the insurer is no longer bound to approve treatment whenever its benefit exceeds the cost. Instead, the threshold value for the treatment decision is determined in competition. Assume that any possible level of $\hat{b}$ can be implemented through an observable contract with a third party reviewer. Generally, insurers may have an incentive to collude on their standards for utilization review by setting the threshold value above the competitive level (where $\hat{b} = c$).

As shown by Bernheim and Whinston (1985), firms can establish collusion by contracting with a common agent (in this case, the review firm). To implement the co-operative outcome, bilateral contracts need not be contingent on the agent's contractual agreements with other firms. Moreover, there is an equilibrium where all strategic variables are set at the co-operative level, even those which are not delegated. It would be interesting to apply this type of model to the present situation.

2.5.3 Utilization Review as a Device for Risk Selection

Managed care organizations are usually compensated on a community-rated basis, implying that insurance premiums do not reflect consumers' individual health risks. In the United States, most non-elderly people receive health insurance coverage through their employer (or a family member's employer). The majority of employers, however, do not adjust workers' premium contributions for differences in expected health care costs.[25] Therefore, for example, the insurer receives the same premium for an old worker as for a young one.[26]

Under community rating, insurers clearly have an incentive to practice risk selection. It is often mentioned that managed care as such induces a favorable self-selection of consumers.[27] Typically, individuals with pre-existing health risks value free provider choice and direct access to specialist treatment more than low-risk consumers do. Therefore, high-risk types are relatively less likely to enroll in managed care, as opposed to traditional health insurance. This will be the case even

[25] See Keenan et al. (2001).

[26] In the US Medicare system, which covers the elderly population, a relatively sophisticated risk adjustment scheme is applied. However, risk adjustment is still imperfect, such that not all predictable differences in individual health care costs are compensated.

[27] See Glied (2000).

if managed care does not involve additional service distortions aimed at attracting good risks.

Additionally, utilization review could be used to ration health care according to consumers' risk types. Insurers have an incentive to selectively deny treatment to consumers whom they expect to be high risks in the longer run. This is consistent with the literature on risk selection: there is wide agreement that insurers try to avoid consumers who generate expected losses, but only if these losses are substantial and of long-term nature.[28]

This type of behavior could be captured by adding a second period to the above model, where individuals differ in their expected costs. Suppose that consumers are still identical ex ante, and have the same treatment cost in the first period of the game. However, the patient's condition in the first period may also be an indicator for future costs. For example, a patient who needs treatment due to an accident or an acute disease typically represents a better risk than one who has developed a chronic condition. In the review process, the insurer may obtain some information on the expected cost of the second period which is not reflected in the present treatment cost or benefit. By denying treatment, some high-risk consumers may probably be "dumped". For instance, some of these individuals may switch to another insurance plan in the next period.

In conclusion, risk selection by managed care organizations deserves further attention. Whether managed care can be seen as a successful innovation depends crucially on how its costs savings are achieved - by selecting profitable risks or by raising the efficiency of health care provision.

2.6 Conclusion

Managed care organizations are often criticized for their utilization review practices. This paper has shown that the criticism is at least partly justified: although utilization review is helpful to implement the ex post efficient treatment decision, it also reduces physicians' incentives to diagnose and subsequently refer patients to specialist treatment. However, the model implies that utilization review raises social welfare if the insurer's commitment problem can be solved.

[28] See, for example, van Barneveld et al. (2000).

In practice, insurers may be tempted to deny coverage in cases where (a higher level of) treatment would be efficient. For instance, there may be profits from selecting favorable risks, or from colluding with other managed care organizations. In this context, commitment to a review strategy does not have a disciplining effect. Instead, external regulation of utilization review firms can be helpful to prevent unjustified denials, but involves additional costs.

Utilization review can also have other advantages apart from reducing the overconsumption of health care services. In particular, it may help avoid unnecessary variation in medical practice styles. As mentioned by Dranove and Spier (2003), a professional reviewer may sometimes be better informed on the effectiveness of different types of treatment than is a primary care physician. Thus, utilization review can be helpful to align medical decision making with scientific evidence. It is not clear, however, what the reviewer's role should be in this context. For instance, it may be optimal to allow the physician to consult an external expert before making a referral decision. These issues may be addressed in future research work.

2.A Proofs

2.A.1 Proofs for the Case without Utilization Review

Concavity of the Insurer's Problem

We consider the case without utilization review. It is convenient to multiply equation (2.7) with $g''(e)/f(\hat{b})$. Thus we obtain the implicit function

$$\Omega(m,\theta,e(m,\theta)) = \frac{e}{\theta}\left(c-\hat{b}\right)g''(e) - \frac{1-F(\hat{b})}{f(\hat{b})}\int_{\hat{b}}^{\bar{b}}[(1-\theta)b-(c-m)]\,dF(b)$$

where $\hat{b} = m/\theta$, and $e(m,\theta)$ is defined by equation (2.1).

Differentiation with respect to m yields:

$$\frac{d\Omega}{dm} = \frac{\partial e}{\partial m}\frac{c-\hat{b}}{\theta}\left[g''(e)+e\,g'''(e)\right] - \frac{e}{\theta^2}\,g''(e) - \left(\frac{1-F(\hat{b})}{f(\hat{b})}\right)'\frac{1}{\theta}\frac{\partial W}{\partial e}$$
$$-\frac{1-F(\hat{b})}{f(\hat{b})}\left[\frac{c-\hat{b}}{\theta}f(\hat{b})+1-F(\hat{b})\right]$$

This expression is negative whenever $\hat{b} < c$. As it cannot be optimal to raise the threshold value above the treatment cost, the problem has a unique solution.

Proof of Remark 1

From the implicit function theorem, it follows that the derivative $dm^*/d\theta$ takes the same sign as the following expression:

$$\frac{d\Omega}{d\theta} = -\frac{e}{\theta^2}(c-\hat{b})\,g''(e) + \frac{e}{\theta^2}\,\hat{b}\,g''(e) + \frac{\partial e}{\partial \theta}\frac{c-\hat{b}}{\theta}\left[g''(e)+e\,g'''(e)\right]$$
$$+\left(\frac{1-F(\hat{b})}{f(\hat{b})}\right)'\frac{\hat{b}}{\theta}\frac{\partial W}{\partial e} + \frac{1-F(\hat{b})}{f(\hat{b})}\left((c-\hat{b})\,f(\hat{b})\,\frac{\hat{b}}{\theta} + \int_{\hat{b}}^{\bar{b}} b\,dF(b)\right)$$

Only the first summand is negative. It can be replaced using the first-order condition (2.7):

$$-\frac{e}{\theta^2}(c-\hat{b})\,g''(e) = -\frac{1-F(\hat{b})}{f(\hat{b})}\frac{1}{\theta}\int_{\hat{b}}^{\bar{b}}\left[(1-\theta)b-(c-m)\right]dF(b)$$

It is easy to see that the following inequality holds whenever $\theta > 1/2$:

$$\int_{\hat{b}}^{\bar{b}}\left[(1-\theta)b-(c-m)\right]dF(b) < \int_{\hat{b}}^{\bar{b}} b\,dF(b)$$

It follows that $dm^*/d\theta > 0$. Taking the derivative with respect to the threshold value $\hat{b}$, it can be shown that $\theta > 1/2$ is also a sufficient condition for $\hat{b}$ to be increasing in the agency parameter.

Moreover, the envelope theorem implies that:

$$\frac{dW}{d\theta} = -e\,(c-\hat{b})f(\hat{b})\frac{m}{\theta^2} + \lambda \int_{\hat{b}}^{\bar{b}} b\,dF(b)$$

Using equation (2.5) to substitute for λ, we obtain, for $dW/d\theta$:

$$-e\,(c-\hat{b})f(\hat{b})\,\frac{m}{\theta^2} + \frac{1}{g''(e)}\left(\int_{\hat{b}}^{\bar{b}} [(1-\theta)b-(c-m)]\,dF(b)\right)\left(\int_{\hat{b}}^{\bar{b}} b\,dF(b)\right)$$

Again, we can apply the first-order condition (2.7):

$$\frac{1}{g''(e)}\left(\int_{\hat{b}}^{\bar{b}} [(1-\theta)b-(c-m)]\,dF(b)\right)\left(\int_{\hat{b}}^{\bar{b}} b\,dF(b) - \hat{b}[1-F(\hat{b})]\right) > 0$$

This completes the proof.

2.A.2 Proofs for the General Case

Concavity of the Insurer's Problem

To prove Proposition 2, it is sufficient to show that the second derivatives d^2W/dm^2 and d^2W/da^2 are negative. In the case with commitment, the first-order condition for the choice of m can be written as

$$\frac{e}{\theta}\left[(c-\hat{b})(1-a)+h(a)\right]g''(e) - \left(\int_{\hat{b}}^{\bar{b}} [(1-\theta)b-c+m]\,dF(b) - \right.$$

$$\left. a\int_{\hat{b}}^{c} [(1-\theta)b-c+m]dF(b) - [1-F(\hat{b})]h(a)\right)\frac{1-F(\hat{b})-a[F(c)-F(\hat{b})]}{f(\hat{b})}$$

which must be equal to zero.

The second derivative is given by:

$$\frac{d^2W}{dm^2} = \frac{\partial e}{\partial m} \frac{(c-\hat{b})(1-a)+h(a)}{\theta} \left[g''(e)+e\,g'''(e)\right] - \frac{e}{\theta^2}(1-a)\,g''(e)$$
$$- \left(\frac{1-F(\hat{b})-a[F(c)-F(\hat{b})]}{f(\hat{b})}\right)' \frac{1}{\theta}\frac{\partial W}{\partial e}$$
$$- \left(1-F(\hat{b})-a[F(c)-F(\hat{b})]\right)\left[(c-\hat{b})(1-a)+h(a)\right]\frac{1}{\theta}$$
$$- \left(1-F(\hat{b})-a[F(c)-F(\hat{b})]\right)^2 / f(\hat{b}) < 0$$

This is negative whenever $\hat{b} = \frac{m}{\theta} < c$. Moreover, the first-order condition for the choice of a takes the form:

$$e\,g''(e)\left(\int_{\hat{b}}^{c}(c-b)\,dF(b) - [1-F(\hat{b})]\,h'(a)\right) - \left(\int_{\hat{b}}^{\bar{b}}[(1-\theta)b-c+m]\,dF(b) - \right.$$
$$\left. a\int_{\hat{b}}^{c}[(1-\theta)b-c+m]\,dF(b) - [1-F(\hat{b})]\,h(a)\right)\int_{\hat{b}}^{c}(\theta b-m)\,dF(b)$$

Differentiation yields:

$$\frac{d^2W}{da^2} = -e\,g''(e)\,[1-F(\hat{b})]\,h''(a) + \int_{\hat{b}}^{c}(\theta b-m)\,dF(b)$$
$$\left(\int_{\hat{b}}^{c}[(1-\theta)b-c+m]\,dF(b) - [1-F(\hat{b})]\,h'(a)\right)$$
$$+\frac{\partial e}{\partial a}\left[g''(e)+e\,g'''(e)\right]\left(\int_{\hat{b}}^{c}(c-b)\,dF(b) - [1-F(\hat{b})]\,h'(a)\right) < 0$$

Example

In the following, we give the most important calculations for the example with the uniform distribution. The effort cost functions are denoted by:

$$g(e) = \frac{\phi_e}{2}\,e^2; \qquad h(a) = \frac{\phi_a}{2}\,a^2$$

In the case without commitment (Case 1), we have:

$$a = \frac{\left(c - \frac{m}{\theta}\right)^2}{\left[2\phi_a \left(1 - \frac{m}{\theta}\right)\right]}$$

$$e = \frac{\theta}{2\,\phi_e}\left[\left(1 - \frac{m}{\theta}\right)^2 - a\left(c - \frac{m}{\theta}\right)^2\right]$$

$$\frac{\partial W}{\partial m} = \frac{e}{\theta}\left[\left(c - \frac{m}{\theta}\right)(1-a) + \frac{\phi_a}{2}a^2\right]$$

$$\frac{\partial W}{\partial e} = \left(1 - \frac{m}{\theta}\right)\left(\frac{1}{2} + \frac{m}{2\theta} - c - \frac{\phi_a}{2}a^2\right) + \frac{a}{2}\left(c - \frac{m}{\theta}\right)^2 - \phi_e\, e$$

$$\frac{\partial W}{\partial a} = e\left[\frac{1}{2}\left(c - \frac{m}{\theta}\right)^2 - \left(1 - \frac{m}{\theta}\right)\phi_a\, a\right]$$

$$\frac{\partial e}{\partial m} = -\frac{1}{\phi_e}\left[\left(1 - \frac{m}{\theta}\right) - a\left(c - \frac{m}{\theta}\right)\right]$$

$$\frac{\partial e}{\partial a} = -\frac{\theta}{2\,\phi_e}\left(c - \frac{m}{\theta}\right)^2$$

$$\frac{\partial a}{\partial m} = -\frac{1}{\theta\,\phi_a}\left(\frac{\left(c - \frac{m}{\theta}\right)}{\left(1 - \frac{m}{\theta}\right)} - \frac{\left(c - \frac{m}{\theta}\right)^2}{2\left(1 - \frac{m}{\theta}\right)^2}\right)$$

In contrast, in Case 2, the insurer's effort choice is characterized by:

$$a = \frac{\left(c - \frac{m}{\theta}\right)(c - m)}{\phi_a \left(1 - \frac{m}{\theta}\right)}$$

$$\frac{\partial a}{\partial m} = -\frac{1}{\phi_a}\left(\frac{(1-c)(c-m)}{\theta\left(1 - \frac{m}{\theta}\right)^2} + \frac{\left(c - \frac{m}{\theta}\right)}{\left(1 - \frac{m}{\theta}\right)}\right)$$

In the case with commitment, the first-order condition for the insurer's effort choice can be solved to obtain $a = 1/2\,|p| - \sqrt{(p^2/4) - q}$, where:

$$|p| = \frac{(2+\theta)\left(c - \frac{m}{\theta}\right)^2}{3\,\phi_a\left(1 - \frac{m}{\theta}\right)} + \frac{2\left(1 - \frac{m}{\theta}\right)^2}{3\left(c - \frac{m}{\theta}\right)^2}; \qquad q = \frac{2}{3\phi_a}\left[c - \frac{m}{\theta} + \frac{\theta}{2}\left(1 - \frac{m}{\theta}\right)\right]$$

The numerical results have been calculated using Matlab.

Chapter 3

Does Risk Adjustment Always Reduce Incentives for Cream Skimming?

3.1 Introduction

Risk selection has been among the most heavily debated issues in health economics during the last years. One of the main reasons is that many countries have implemented social health insurance systems which, on the one hand, rely on competition, but, on the other hand, are aimed at treating individuals with different health risks equally. To reach this goal, insurers are prohibited from setting differentiated premiums based on consumers' risk categories. This regulation, however, gives incentives for cream skimming, that is, for direct and indirect risk selection. By direct selection, we understand insurers' attempts to accept only those applicants for whom expected costs are below revenue, based on insurer information. Indirect selection, which is related to the phenomenon of adverse selection, implies that insurers attract low-risk consumers by rationing some services more than others.

To prevent cream skimming, insurers are usually required to enroll all applicants regardless of their risk type and to offer a regulated benefit package. Moreover, in many countries, premium payments are adjusted to compensate for differences in insurers' risk structures. Risk adjustment is currently used in over 20 countries (including Australia, Germany, the Netherlands, Switzerland, Israel and the Medicare sector in the US). However, existing risk adjustment models predict future health care costs only imperfectly and do not sufficiently reduce incentives for cream skimming. Therefore, insurers may still make substantial profits if they can exploit private information to select preferred risks.

Although current risk adjustment methods, which often only account for age and sex of the insured, have been frequently criticized, there is wide agreement that these payment schemes are at least superior to a system without risk adjustment. The premise behind this argument is that "more information is always better" in the design of a risk adjustment scheme, in the sense of Blackwell's theorem.[1] The present paper shows that this may not be the case if the information needed by the insurer to practice risk selection is costly to obtain. Surprisingly, *imperfect* risk adjustment may instead raise incentives for cream skimming.

Two assumptions are necessary to derive this result. Firstly, direct risk selection can be practiced to some extent, and secondly, the insurer's private information is endogenous. Since the regulatory framework involves open enrollment, explicit rejection of unprofitable consumers is not possible. However, insurers can use other strategies to select preferred risks. For instance, they may process applications of high-risk individuals only slowly, or engage insurance agents who advise unprofitable consumers to enroll with another company. This type of behavior is not contractible and cannot be directly observed by the regulator.

In some countries, such as the Netherlands and Switzerland, social health insurance is provided by firms which also offer supplementary insurance at a risk-based premium. There is concern that insurers may deny supplementary coverage to consumers with high health risks. As most consumers prefer to obtain health insurance from a single firm, they will probably switch to another insurer in this case. More generally, the possibility to tie (basic) health insurance to other insurance products represents a powerful selection tool.

Another problem observed in Switzerland is that insurers may form conglomerates, which effectively enables them to set risk-dependent premiums. For this purpose, insurance agents transfer the worst risks to the firm with the highest premium, whereas the most favorable risks are enrolled by the cheapest insurer. Although

[1] See Blackwell (1951).

these strategies are not explicitly considered here, the model can be interpreted to capture these situations as well.[2]

In the following, it is assumed that the regulator and the insurer can initially observe the same information on a consumer's risk type, which may be used in the payment scheme. Alternatively, there may be no risk adjustment. By exerting an effort, the insurer can observe additional risk factors, which enables him to identify (and possibly avoid) applicants for whom the expected health care costs exceed the risk-adjusted payment. In practice, insurers may look into patients' medical histories or existing diagnoses, and collect information on family health histories or regional differences in expenditure. Even if it is not allowed to ask questions related to an applicant's health status, insurers may obtain this type of information through contact with insurance agents or, possibly, with medical providers.[3]

Clearly, the incentive to acquire private information depends on the compensation scheme. Without risk adjustment, the insurer tries to avoid consumers with "unfavorable" observable characteristics (for example, elderly people). If these risk factors are accounted for in the payment scheme, there will be no more discrimination against these groups. However, the marginal benefit of information is generally higher under risk adjustment. Accordingly, the insurer will try even harder to screen out high risks *within* given cost groups (here, age groups). This has ambiguous welfare effects: the model shows that both the proportion of individuals who are affected by the insurer's selection activities and the potential profit from selection may be higher under *imperfect* risk adjustment.

It is important to notice that the incentive for cream skimming depends on the accuracy of risk adjustment in a discontinuous way. A perfect risk adjustment scheme would be one which predicted individual treatment costs as accurately as this is technically possible. Thus, the insurer could no longer identify profitable subgroups of consumers, and there would be no incentive for selection. However, a highly imperfect scheme may reduce social welfare.

[2] Van de Ven and Schut (2007) describe the situation in the Netherlands and Beck et al. (2006) that in Switzerland. Of course, governments could also try to reduce selection by additional regulation, such as preventing any contact between consumers and insurance agents, or prohibiting tied sales. The problem here is that some measures which could reduce selection would also reduce competition. Moreover, the *incentive* for selection would not be removed.

[3] Van de Ven and Schut (2007) also mention informational costs as one type of selection costs incurred by insurers.

This argument is closely related to a paper by Sappington and Lewis (1999). The authors analyze how information acquisition by an insurer affects the optimal payment scheme to prevent risk selection. Assuming that payments are based on the insurer's report on individual risk types, they find that it may be optimal to prevent the insurer from collecting any private information. If this is the case, finer risk adjustment is not always desirable because it can raise procurement costs. In contrast to the present paper, Sappington and Lewis assume that through risk adjustment, new information is released which aggravates the incentive problem between the regulator and the insurer. They argue that *observable* characteristics such as age and sex should always be accounted for in the payment scheme.

In contrast to this, the result of the present paper is valid when risk adjustment reduces the regulator's informational disadvantage relative to the insurer. As the result is derived in a context of statistical risk adjustment, it also has important practical implications. As mentioned, statistical or "conventional" risk adjustment implies that the insurer is compensated for predictable differences in individual treatment costs. This, however, does not necessarily correspond to an optimal payment scheme.

We also address the question of *how* the payment scheme should be designed. For this purpose, we consider a similar compensation structure as in Sappington and Lewis (1999). In particular, part of individual health care expenditure may be reimbursed by the regulator. As the reimbursement rates are conditional on the insurer's information on consumers' risk types, this is part of an optimal revelation mechanism. While cost sharing lowers the incentive for selection, it also has a negative effect on efficiency. This trade-off can be improved if information acquisition is allowed to some extent. Assuming that the level of information can be continuously chosen, the insurer always obtains some private information in equilibrium. This result is in contrast to Sappington and Lewis. Moreover, the optimal payment scheme typically involves elements of cost sharing as well as statistical risk adjustment.

Several other authors have suggested specific incentive schemes to reduce risk selection. In particular, Glazer and McGuire (2000) show that indirect selection can be prevented by overcompensating the insurer for differences in expected treatment costs. Marchand et al. (2000) consider a two-period model with direct selection. Here, cost sharing based on prior health care expenditure may also be useful because this variable may be correlated with the insurers' private information at the enrollment stage. Kifmann and Lorenz (2005) derive an optimal non-linear cost reimbursement function. Their paper especially provides an argument against so-called outlier cost sharing. This may be counterproductive if low-risk consumers are more likely than other risk types to have very low *or* very high illness severities. Finally, Barros (2003) proposes an ex post equalization fund to compensate for differences in insurers' risk structures.[4]

Research on *statistical* risk adjustment is primarily aimed at finding the right combination of variables (also referred to as risk adjusters) to be included in the payment scheme. The intention is to raise the predictive power of the risk adjustment model, without relying on certain variables which are hard to collect or which are ruled out for some other reasons. For example, it may not be desirable to make payments conditional on individual characteristics such as lifestyle or preventive behavior, or on regional characteristics such as the density of health care providers.[5] Van de Ven and Ellis (2000) summarize the criteria for a "good" risk adjuster. The exclusion of undesirable risk adjusters is one reason why insurers can usually predict individual expenditure more precisely than the regulator can.

A few studies are concerned with estimating insurers' potential profits from cream skimming. Shen and Ellis (2002) compare the profits attainable under different risk adjustment schemes, when the insurer can use alternative information sets to predict individual health care costs. They find that all current methods still leave substantial gains to insurers. For instance, the best available risk adjustment model, based on diagnostic information, is able to reduce potential profits by about one half. A weakness of this approach is that the authors do not consider any costs of selection, nor any regulatory limits.

Van Barneveld et al. (2000) argue that insurers treat consumers with small predictable losses or profits neutrally. This is because discrimination against or in favor of these groups entails additional costs, particularly in the form of reputational losses. Moreover, small expected losses or profits may be due to random variations and do not play an important role in the long run. The authors show that the incentive for risk selection is overestimated if this aspect is neglected.

[4] See also the discussion in Section 3.4.

[5] Variables which can be easily manipulated should not be taken into account, either. Nevertheless, German social health insurers do receive transfer payments for consumers who participate in disease management programs aimed at chronically ill patients. Thus, there is an incentive to enroll fairly healthy consumers in these programs.

Beck et al. (2006) define an effective risk adjustment scheme as one which sufficiently reduces the proportion of consumers who generate *substantial* expected profits or losses, given the insurer's information. Using data from Switzerland, they show that the current risk adjustment scheme (based on age and sex) does not sufficiently reduce incentives for cream skimming. This is justified by the argument that possible cost savings due to selection are still more important under this scheme than are savings due to investments in cost efficiency (such as managed care).

The rest of the paper is structured as follows. The model is presented in the next section. Section 3.3 is concerned with statistical risk adjustment, which is shown to have ambiguous welfare effects. In Section 3.4, the optimal payment scheme with cost sharing based on insurer information is derived. Section 3.5 concludes.

3.2 The Model

There are three kinds of players in the model: consumers, a regulator who purchases health insurance coverage for the consumer population, and an insurer. To keep the model as simple as possible, we abstract from competition and consider only a single, profit-maximizing insurer. This seems to be a reasonable assumption, although in a social health insurance system, firms may not directly pursue profit maximization: to ensure their economic survival, insurers want to accumulate reserves, which effectively implies a behavior equivalent to maximizing (discounted) expected profits.[6]

In principle, the model can be applied to a wider range of situations where risk selection is problematic. For example, the insurer might be interpreted as a health care provider (a hospital or a group of physicians) paid by capitation. Here, the provider bears the financial risk caused by any heterogeneity in the patient population which is not reflected in the payment scheme.

Consumers do not make any direct premium payments to the insurer. Instead, the regulator collects a uniform contribution payment from every individual, denoted by z, which is based on average health risk. The insurer, in turn, receives a transfer for each enrolled consumer. Depending on the compensation scheme,

[6] See also Zweifel (2005).

the regulator may also reimburse part of individual expenditure.[7] Moreover, we assume that all consumers can be committed to participate in the social health insurance system. This especially involves the cross-subsidization between different risk types.

There are two types of consumers: high risks and low risks, indexed by $i = h, l$. The proportion of each risk type is given by p_i, and the population size is normalized to one. Each type is characterized by its specific distribution of health care costs over a given time period. For our purposes, it is sufficient to distinguish the two types with respect to their expected costs. In the absence of insurer effort, the cost levels are given by k_i, where $k_h > k_l$. Any further variation in individual expenditure is purely random and cannot be predicted ex ante. The expected cost is given by $\bar{k} = p_h k_h + p_l k_l$.

Realized treatment costs also depend on the insurer's cost reduction effort e, which is a continuous variable. This can be interpreted as the insurer's effort in monitoring health care providers, or in negotiating favorable contractual terms with them. For simplicity, we assume that the impact of e on expected treatment costs is similar for both risk types:[8]

$$c_h(e) = k_h - e; \qquad c_l(e) = k_l - e$$

The effort cost per insured consumer is described by the function $g(e)$, which is strictly increasing and convex, $g'(e) > 0$ and $g''(e) > 0$. To ensure that the socially optimal effort level and the expected costs of both risk types are strictly positive, we also assume that $g'(0) = 0$ and $g'(k_l) > 1$. Another simplification here is to assume constant returns to scale with respect to the number of enrolled consumers. Thus there is no direct interaction between the insurer's cost reduction effort and his selection activities.

[7] This indirect compensation scheme reflects the situation in countries such as Belgium and the Netherlands. In practice, insurers may charge an additional, community-rated premium. The premium covers only a relatively small part of average expenditure, but allows for price competition at the margin. This system is believed to be relatively transparent because price differences between insurers become more obvious to consumers. A similar system, known as *Gesundheitsfonds*, has recently been introduced in Germany.

[8] For a similar assumption, see Marchand et al. (2000) or Sappington and Lewis (1999). Empirically, the effect of insurer effort on expenditure has been shown to exist, with savings being at least as large for high risks as for low risks. See Felder and Beck (1999).

The regulator does not know consumers' risk types, but can observe some characteristics which are correlated with the underlying type. This information is represented by the binary signal $s = 1, 0$. In general, the signal might be anything from a readily observable characteristic (age, sex) to a clinical diagnosis. Here, the signal can be initially observed by the insurer as well. The conditional probability of s is denoted by $p_{s|i}$, where $p_{1|h} > p_{1|l}$. Thus the probability of facing a high-risk type is larger upon observing signal 1 than in the case of signal 0.[9] According to Bayes' rule, the posterior probabilities are given by:

$$p_{i|1} = \frac{p_i p_{1|i}}{p_1}; \qquad p_{i|0} = \frac{p_i p_{0|i}}{p_0}$$

Moreover, we define $p_s = p_h p_{s|h} + p_l p_{s|l}$. The expected cost levels conditional on $s = 0, 1$ are characterized by $k_s = p_{h|s} k_h + p_{l|s} k_l$, where $k_1 > \bar{k} > k_0$.

Drawing an analogy between the signal and a diagnostic test, we can define $p_{1|h}$ and $p_{0|l}$ as sensitivity and specificity of the signal, respectively. In contrast, $p_{l|1}$ and $p_{h|0}$ represent the probabilities of a type I error and type II error. These are related to the predictive power of the signal.

As mentioned, the insurer may obtain some private information. This is modeled in the following way: upon observing the signal s, the insurer chooses a probability a_s with which he may discover an applicant's true risk type.[10] The cost of information acquisition is described by the function $f(a)$, which satisfies the standard properties $f'(a) > 0$, $f''(a) > 0$ and $f'(0) = 0$. Moreover, the corner solution of complete information can be avoided if $f'(1)$ is sufficiently large. We consider two alternative assumptions regarding the information structure:

Assumption 1 *If the search for information is successful, which occurs with probability a, the insurer can directly observe an individual's risk type.*

Assumption 2 *If facing an h-type, the insurer finds out about this with probability a. In contrast, no additional information can be found about the l-type.*

9 For example, if the signal is interpreted as age, $s = 0$ stands for a young person, whereas $s = 1$ represents the elderly.

10 This technology has been introduced by Aghion and Tirole (1997). In the context of risk selection, a similar assumption is considered by Eggleston (2000).

Figures 3.1 and 3.2 illustrate the insurer's decision under both assumptions. Assumption 2 reflects the possibility that high risks may be easier to detect than low risks. For instance, they may show specific disease symptoms or an unfavorable health behavior. If no such risk factors can be observed, the insurer does not know whether his investigations were unsuccessful, or whether he is facing a low risk. Being aware of this, he updates his expectations. Expected costs are given by:

$$E[k_x|s] = \frac{p_{h|s}(1-a_s)k_h + p_{l|s}k_l}{p_{h|s}(1-a_s) + p_{l|s}}$$

This value determines whether enrolling the consumer is profitable from the insurer's point of view.

Risk selection itself is modeled in a stylized way. Initially, the insurer faces an average consumer population seeking enrollment. After further investigating individuals' health risks, he tries to reject those applicants whom he considers unprofitable. For instance, he may skimp on service quality (including friendliness of staff or timely processing of applications), or convince applicants to obtain insurance coverage from another firm. Consumers' reaction is taken into account by assuming that a proportion $\phi_i \in [0,1)$ of applicants who are affected by this negative discrimination still decide to enroll with the insurer, while the others switch to an outside option. The proportion ϕ_i is taken as exogenous. It may generally depend on the risk type, although in the present context, consumers need not be fully aware of their own type. Moreover, we assume that individuals cannot be completely "dumped" from the social health insurance system.[11]

The utility loss of an individual who is affected by the insurer's selection activities is defined equal to v_i. This parameter represents the utility derived from health insurance in the absence of selection.[12] We assume that the insurer incurs no further selection costs, apart from the informational cost. Certainly, it would be desirable to model risk selection in an explicit way, for instance, as a distortion in service quality. While such an extension would be possible, it would also make the analysis more complicated. The present approach has the advantage that the incentive for

[11] See the discussion in Section 3.3.4.

[12] More precisely, utility losses may differ between those consumers who switch to another firm and those who enroll despite the insurer's attempt for selection. This distinction would not have an important effect on the model results.

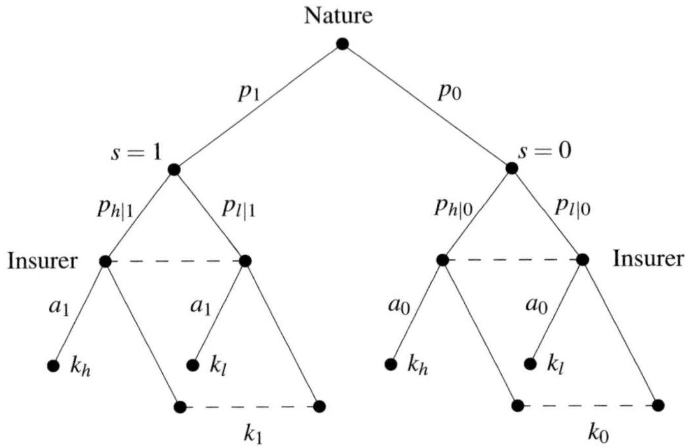

Figure 3.1: Information structure under Assumption 1.

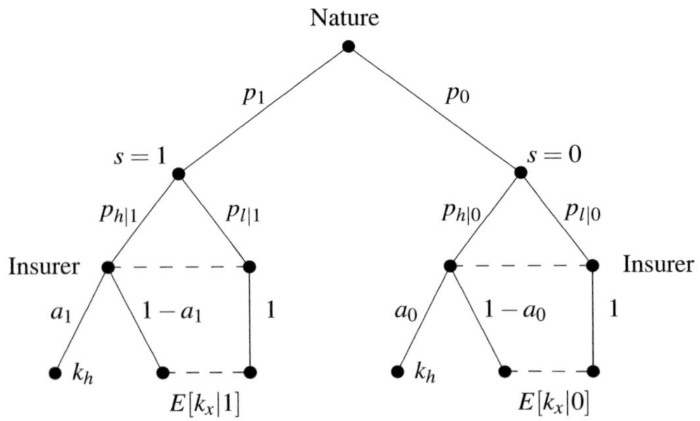

Figure 3.2: Information structure under Assumption 2.

selection, measured by the potential profit, can be represented in a general form. This is independent of the instruments which are used for cream skimming.[13]

The time structure of the model is the following. First, the regulator offers a payment scheme, which is accepted by the insurer in equilibrium. Then, the insurer chooses an effort for cost reduction. This should be thought of as a long-run choice because it concerns the organizational structure of health insurance. At the enrollment stage, the insurer observes the consumer's signal and chooses an effort for information acquisition. Based on the observed information, the enrollment decision is made. Treatment costs are realized at the ex post stage.

3.3 Statistical Risk Adjustment

When health insurers are compensated using statistical risk adjustment, the regulator's aim is to predict consumers' expected costs as accurately as possible, without including certain variables which are considered as unsuitable. For each consumer, the insurer effectively receives a payment equal to the predicted cost. In the following, statistical risk adjustment, based on a given set of variables (here, the signal s), is compared to a reference case where the regulator chooses to ignore this information. The analysis is positive in nature. We take the available payment schemes as given and analyze their effects on the insurer's behavior and on social welfare. Here, only the (more general) information structure of Assumption 1 is considered. It can be shown that the results carry over to the other case as well.

3.3.1 Cost Efficiency

The payment schemes considered in this section belong to the class of prospective payment systems. Accordingly, the transfers to the insurer - denoted by t_0 and t_1 - may depend on the signal s, but not on realized costs. Assuming that the cost estimates underlying these payments can be calculated on a prospective basis, cost efficiency remains undistorted.

[13] Since we are concerned with the organizational framework of health insurance, we abstract from risk aversion. This is standard in the literature on risk selection. See, for example, Glazer and McGuire (2000) and Kifmann (2002).

Proposition 1 *Under a prospective payment scheme, the insurer chooses the socially optimal effort level e^*.*

The proof is straightforward. For every enrolled consumer, the insurer obtains an expected profit of:

$$t_s - k_i + e - g(e)$$

The effort level is chosen such as to minimize total costs, and the first-order condition is given by $g'(e^*) = 1$. Clearly, this is in line with social efficiency. This result allows us to abstract from cost efficiency issues and to focus on the insurer's enrollment decision for the remainder of this section.

We assume that the transfer payments are determined in such a way that the insurer makes zero profit *without* risk selection.[14] In the system with risk adjustment, labeled by *RA*, the payment amounts to:

$$t_s^{RA} = k_s - e^* + g(e^*)$$

In the reference case, labeled by *N*, the insurer receives a uniform payment for every consumer:

$$t_s^N = \bar{k} - e^* + g(e^*)$$

Thus in the absence of risk adjustment, there is one profitable group of consumers ($s = 0$), whereas the other group ($s = 1$) brings losses, on average.

3.3.2 Enrollment Decision

In the following, we discuss the insurer's selection strategy in more detail. The aim is to clarify the role of the self-selection parameter ϕ_i.

If the insurer is fully informed, he enrolls all low-risk individuals and tries to reject as many high-risk consumers as possible. In contrast, if only the signal is observable, and if there is no risk adjustment, one might expect that the insurer tries to deter consumers with signal 1. This, however, depends on the consumers' reaction to the insurer's selection behavior. The following assumptions regarding ϕ_i

[14] See Eggleston (2000) for a similar approach.

are made:[15]

$$(1-\phi_h)p_{1|h} \geq (1-\phi_l)p_{1|l} \tag{3.1}$$

$$(1-\phi_h)p_{0|h} \leq (1-\phi_l)p_{0|l} \tag{3.2}$$

If the first inequality is violated, there is a large probability that high-risk consumers will enroll with the insurer even if they observe a low quality of service or some other selection behavior. In contrast, the low-risk type is relatively likely to switch. Due to this unfavorable self-selection, the insurer would prefer to encourage enrollment even if $s = 1$. As we are concerned with direct risk selection, we assume that the self-selection effect is not too strong, i.e., that inequality (3.1) holds. Similarly, inequality (3.2) guarantees that the insurer treats individuals with $s = 0$ at least neutrally.

Under risk adjustment, the insurer just breaks even with each signal type. Thus if $\phi_l > \phi_h$, it would be profitable to discourage enrollment unless the consumer's exact risk type is known. This, however, seems quite unrealistic. Although not explicitly considered here, there might be adverse selection into health insurance in addition to direct risk selection (implying that $\phi_h > \phi_l$). Low-risk consumers who are erroneously rejected can indeed expect a better service, or better conditions for supplementary insurance, from another insurer on average. Finally, if the insurer is willing to forgo a small selection profit (e.g., due to reputational concerns), a small self-selection effect in either direction does not play a role.

Under these assumptions, risk adjustment is desirable a priori because it makes consumers with signal 1 better off. However, the payment scheme also affects the insurer's decision on information acquisition, which again determines the total probability of selection. This is analyzed in Section 3.3.3.

3.3.3 Information Acquisition

We first consider the insurer's choice of informational effort a in the absence of risk adjustment. If signal 0 is observed, additional information is valuable only if the individual turns out to be a high risk. In this case, the insurer changes his selection

[15] The following expressions are derived in more detail in the Appendix 3.A.

strategy and tries to reject the applicant. In contrast, the low-risk type is always enrolled. It can be shown that the first-order condition for information acquisition is given by:

$$f'(a_0^N) = p_{h|0}\, p_l\, (1-\phi_h)(k_h - k_l) \tag{3.3}$$

The incentive to acquire information is increasing in the probability of falsely enrolling a high-risk individual ($p_{h|0}$). Moreover, it is positively related to the cost difference $k_h - k_l$, which measures the financial benefit of selection, and to the probability that a high-risk consumer can be avoided $(1-\phi_h)$. Finally, for a given signal distribution, the marginal benefit of information is maximal at $p_h = p_l = \frac{1}{2}$, where the initial uncertainty on the risk type is highest.[16]

As a consumer with signal 1 is a priori "unprofitable", detecting a high-risk type does not change the insurer's selection strategy in this case. Surprisingly, the benefit of information consists in the possibility of finding a low-risk consumer, who could be falsely rejected otherwise. This is reflected in the first-order condition:

$$f'(a_1^N) = p_h\, p_{l|1}\, (1-\phi_l)(k_h - k_l) \tag{3.4}$$

In contrast to equation (3.3), this depends on the probability of a type I error and on the low risk type's propensity to switch to another insurer when exposed to (negative) selection.

The intuition can be summarized as follows: Under incomplete information, risk selection is based on the signal s. When fully informed, the insurer can make a more accurate decision, thereby trying to avoid high-risk individuals instead of those who *seem* to be high risks. The more these groups overlap, i.e., the more accurate the signal, the more likely will his preferences remain unchanged.

When risk adjustment is introduced, the insurer has an incentive to screen out high risks within each cost group. Conditional on $s = 0, 1$, the first-order conditions are given by:

$$f'(a_s^{RA}) = p_{h|s}\, p_{l|s}\, (1-\phi_h)(k_h - k_l) \tag{3.5}$$

Accordingly, the level of information a_s^{RA} is maximal if the probability of a "false" signal ($p_{l|1}$ or $p_{h|0}$) equals one half. In contrast to the system without risk adjust-

[16] This can be seen when inserting $p_{h|0} = p_h\, p_{0|h}/p_0$.

ment, the benefit of information does not continue to increase with the error probability beyond this point. Clearly, this is because the transfer payments t_s also depend on the error probabilities. Comparing equation (3.5) to the first-order conditions for the N-system yields the following result:

Proposition 2 *If $s = 0$, the insurer becomes informed with a higher probability in the RA-system than in the N-system. If $s = 1$, a sufficient condition for the level of information to be higher under risk adjustment is $\phi_l \geq \phi_h$.*

This follows directly from $p_{l|0} > p_l$ and $p_{h|1} > p_h$. The intuition why the level of information tends to be higher under risk adjustment is straightforward. Again, consider the case $s = 0$ first. The financial gain from rejecting a high-risk consumer is higher under risk adjustment than in the reference case, as $|k_0 - k_h| > |\bar{k} - k_h|$. Thus, avoiding a type II error is rewarded more in the *RA*-system. Similarly, if $s = 1$, the profit margin for a low-risk consumer is higher under risk adjustment, since $k_1 - k_l > \bar{k} - k_l$. This effect tends to raise the level of information.

Proposition 2 has ambiguous implications. As mentioned, consumers with signal 1 are (weakly) better off under risk adjustment. In contrast, high risks who are in the lower compensation group ($s = 0$) prefer the system without risk adjustment, where they face a lower probability of selection. From equation (3.5), we can immediately draw the following conclusion:

Proposition 3 *Under risk adjustment, the insurer's incentive to acquire information decreases as the predictive power of the signal rises. In the limit, the probability of selection goes to zero as $p_{h|1}$ and $p_{l|0}$ tend to one.*

In this sense, the presumption that "more information is always better" is correct. In the *RA*-system, the probability of selection is proportional to the insurer's level of information. Therefore, selection is reduced as the underlying signal becomes more informative. A direct implication is that a sufficiently accurate risk adjustment scheme can always improve social welfare. However, Proposition 3 does not give evidence whether a *given* signal should be used as a risk adjuster. In practice, only imperfect risk adjustment is available, so it is important to consider its welfare effects in more detail.

3.3.4 Welfare Analysis

It is difficult to determine the exact welfare loss from risk selection in a social health insurance system. Selection is a zero-sum game, and any profit accruing to one insurer due to a favorable risk structure corresponds to an equivalent loss for some other firm(s). In a perfectly competitive market, insurers (with otherwise similar characteristics) are forced to adopt a symmetric selection strategy in order to survive. Even in this case, distortions in quality and efficiency will generally arise.[17] Nevertheless, the assumption that positive selection profits are possible seems appropriate if insurers have some market power, or if they differ in their ability to control costs.[18]

Another question related to the welfare function is *why* the government wants to impose community-rated premiums, thereby making risk selection attractive to insurers. This can be justified both on equity and efficiency grounds. Higher premiums for persons with pre-existing health risks are often considered as inequitable, especially if individuals are not responsible for their condition. Moreover, a fair (risk-based) premium would be unaffordable for some consumers, such that universal access to health insurance would no longer be guaranteed. Since the premium risk itself is not insurable, community-rating provides a way to overcome this market failure. As the focus of the paper is on the design of the risk adjustment scheme, we take this policy as given here.[19]

In the following, we assume that the regulator aims to maximize a weighted sum of consumer welfare and insurer profits. To account for equity considerations, the utility of high-risk consumers may have a higher weight in the welfare function than that of low-risk individuals. The weights are denoted by ω_i, where $\omega_h \geq 1$, $\omega_l \leq 1$

[17] For instance, in the shorter run, cream skimming may be used as a substitute for cost-reducing investments if insurers' financial resources are limited. An aggressive selection strategy may allow relatively inefficient firms to survive in the market. Moreover, selection may also create instability due to a continuous exit of insurers.

[18] In Switzerland, for example, the largest health insurers seem to differ significantly in their tendency to practice risk selection. See Beck et al. (2006), p. 57.

[19] Despite the popularity of community-rating, its justification is not straightforward. The regulator's goal could be achieved by a system of premium subsidies, while allowing insurers to charge risk-based premiums. In particular, Zweifel and Breuer (2006) argue in favor of such a system. In a reply to their suggestion, van de Ven (2006) states that premium subsidies distort competition and induce over-insurance of high-risk consumers. Moreover, Kifmann and Roeder (2008) show that in most cases, social health insurance combined with appropriate (non-linear) taxation is superior on equity grounds.

and $p_h \omega_h + p_l \omega_l = 1$. Utility losses may arise because consumers cannot obtain the preferred (basic) insurance coverage, or because they have to obtain supplementary insurance from another firm. Clearly, the expected utility $E[v_i]$ is proportional to the probability that there is *no* discrimination against an individual of type i. Therefore, the source of the utility loss need not be further specified.

In general, profits are also valued by society. As we assume that consumers cannot be completely "dumped" from the social health insurance system, however, selection profits are effectively financed out of public funds. We denote the insurer's gain from selection, excluding informational costs, by $\tilde{\pi}$. Total health care spending is given by $z^* + \tilde{\pi}$, where z^* represents the contribution charged to each consumer in the absence of risk selection. The budget is balanced if $z^* = \bar{k} - e^* + g(e^*)$. In the model framework, this treatment of selection profits can be justified by assuming that individuals who are rejected are transferred to an outside option (e.g., a publicly owned firm), where they are insured at the same expected cost. If the outside firm is less efficient, there will be an additional loss that is proportional to the probability of selection.

As is standard in the literature, we assume that public spending is financed out of distortionary taxes or contribution payments. The marginal cost of public funds is represented by the parameter $\omega_\pi > 0$. In addition, ω_π may reflect a higher negative weight on selection profits. This may be appropriate if part of the insurer's revenue is spent unproductively in order to hide an illegal profit. Altogether, the welfare function is given by:

$$W = \omega_h p_h E[v_h] + \omega_l p_l E[v_l] - (1 + \omega_\pi) z^* - \omega_\pi \tilde{\pi} - E[f(a_s)]$$

The alternative payment schemes can be compared regarding three components: the probability of selection (for both risk types), the insurer's gross profit and the amount of resources spent on selection activities, which is represented by the function $f(a)$. Proposition 4 states the main result of this section.

Proposition 4 *Social welfare may be lower under imperfect risk adjustment than without any risk adjustment. While low risks are unambiguously better off in the RA-system, high risks may face a higher selection probability in the N-system. The comparison of gross profits $\tilde{\pi}$ also yields ambiguous results.*

Arguably, the possibility that high risks may be worse off under risk adjustment raises particular concern, because one of the main goals of social health insurance is to improve the situation of this group. This case applies if:

$$p_{1|h}\,(1-a_1^{RA}) < p_{0|h}\,(a_0^{RA}-a_0^N)$$

Under this condition, the utility loss of individuals with signal 0 more than outweighs the utility gain of those with signal 1. This situation is more likely if the sensitivity of the signal ($p_{1|h}$) is relatively low. Generally, this depends both on the accuracy of the signal and on the signal distribution itself.

We also give the insurer's gross profits, under both payment schemes:

$$\tilde{\pi}^N = \left\{(1-\phi_h)[p_{1|h}+p_{0|h}a_0^N]-(1-\phi_l)p_{1|l}(1-a_1^N)\right\}p_h p_l(k_h-k_l)$$

$$\tilde{\pi}^{RA} = (1-\phi_h)\left(\frac{p_{1|l}p_{1|h}}{p_1}\,a_1^{RA}+\frac{p_{0|l}p_{0|h}}{p_0}\,a_0^{RA}\right)p_h p_l(k_h-k_l)$$

There are two reasons why $\tilde{\pi}$ may be lower in the N-system than in the RA-system. On the one hand, the possibility of falsely rejecting a good risk has a negative effect on $\tilde{\pi}^N$. On the other hand, as mentioned above, risk adjustment raises the selection profit if $s=0$.

Example. An example is helpful to illustrate this result. For convenience, we consider a completely symmetric information structure. That is, $p_h=\frac{1}{2}$ and $p_{h|1}=p_{l|0}\equiv q>\frac{1}{2}$. Moreover, the probability of switching ϕ_i, the weight ω_i and the utility loss from selection v_i are equal for both risk types. The insurer's investigation costs are quadratic, $f(a)=a^2/2$, and we assume that $(1-\phi_h)(k_h-k_l)=4$. Thus the probabilities a_s^{RA} and a_s^N are smaller than one, and the level of information is always higher under risk adjustment.

High risks are better off *without* risk adjustment if:

$$q\,[1-4q(1-q)] < (1-q)\,[4q(1-q)-2(1-q)]$$

$$\Leftrightarrow \quad q^2-\frac{7}{6}q+\frac{1}{3}<0$$

This inequality is fulfilled if the accuracy of the signal is relatively low, $q \in \left(\frac{1}{2}, \frac{2}{3}\right)$, whereas risk adjustment is favorable if $q \in \left(\frac{2}{3}, 1\right)$.

If low-risk consumers are also taken into account, this result does not hold anymore. The corresponding inequality for the whole population is:

$$q\,[1-4q(1-q)] + (1-q)\,[1-2(1-q)] < (1-q)\,[4q(1-q)-2(1-q)]$$

$$\Leftrightarrow \quad 1 < 4q(1-q)$$

This cannot be fulfilled, and holds with equality only if the signal is uninformative ($q=\frac{1}{2}$). However, if low-risk individuals incur a smaller utility loss from selection, or if the utility of the high-risk type is weighted more, there must be a non-empty range of q where risk adjustment reduces consumer welfare (excluding contribution payments). Moreover, the insurer's (gross) profit is higher under risk adjustment if:

$$\tilde{\pi}^N = 4(1-q)^2 + 2q - 1 < 16q^2(1-q)^2 = \tilde{\pi}^{RA}$$

$$\Leftrightarrow \quad \frac{1}{4} < (2q+1)(1-q)^2$$

Here, $q \leq \frac{2}{3}$ is a sufficient condition. Altogether, imperfect risk adjustment reduces social welfare if q is sufficiently close to one half.

The results imply that it is worthwhile looking for variables which are strongly correlated with the underlying risk type. Of course, implementing a more sophisticated risk adjustment scheme also involves a (possibly substantial) transaction cost. The regulator needs to collect more data at the individual consumer level. Moreover, it may be costly to learn the exact relationship between specific risk factors, such as existing diagnoses, and expected treatment costs. Without this effort, however, it may not be possible to provide appropriate incentives to insurers.

3.3.5 Unobservable Information

Here, we consider the case where the signal s is *not* initially observable to the insurer. This implies that the insurer may obtain new information through the payment scheme. Interestingly, this is not problematic in the present context.

Assume that the insurer observes the signal only when receiving the payment t_s, that is, after the consumer has been enrolled. In the system without risk adjustment, the insurer may learn the applicant's true risk type, but s remains unobservable. The first-order condition for the insurer's information acquisition is given by:

$$f'(a^N) = p_h p_l (1-\phi_h)(k_h - k_l) = p_h(1-\phi_h)(k_h - \bar{k}) \tag{3.6}$$

The benefit of information corresponds to the *unconditional* expected profit from avoiding a high risk. In contrast, if risk adjustment is introduced, the insurer's decision is characterized by:

$$f'(a^{RA}) = p_h(1-\phi_h)(k_h - p_{1|h}k_1 - p_{0|h}k_0) \tag{3.7}$$

For a high-risk consumer, the insurer now receives an expected payment equal to $p_{1|h}k_1 - p_{0|h}k_0$. As the signal is informative, this expression exceeds the payment based on expected costs $\bar{k}$.[20] The following conclusion can be made:

Proposition 5 *Statistical risk adjustment unambiguously raises social welfare if the signal s cannot be initially observed by the insurer. Both the probability of selection and the insurer's profit are lower than in the reference case.*[21]

Proposition 5 implies that variables which are difficult to observe for the insurer, such as clinical diagnoses, make better risk adjusters than do observable characteristics. This strengthens the argument in favor of more advanced risk adjustment schemes, for example, based on clinical information.

3.3.6 Outlook

Although the main result of this section, according to which statistical risk adjustment is not always desirable, seems surprising, it can be easily understood from a general economic perspective. As mentioned by Glazer and McGuire (2000, 2006),

[20] Notice that $p_{1|h}k_1 - p_{0|h}k_0 > p_1k_1 + p_0k_0 = \bar{k}$.

[21] The result still applies if the signal becomes observable to the insurer *before* the decision on a is taken. A sufficient condition for Proposition 5 to hold is $f'''(a) \geq 0$. It follows from Jensen's inequality that the average probability of selection (over $s = 0, 1$) must be lower under risk adjustment than in the reference case.

statistical risk adjustment does not reflect an optimization behavior on the regulator's side. If this were the case, Blackwell's theorem could generally be applied.

In the following section, the question of *how* the optimal compensation scheme should be designed is further explored. For this purpose, we do no longer consider the class of purely prospective payment schemes. Under these schemes, the degree of risk selection depends on several probabilities, so that general results regarding the optimal transfers are hard to derive. Moreover, the revelation principle[22] implies that the regulator should extract the insurer's private information on consumers' risk types. This possibility is analyzed in Section 3.4 in a framework of cost sharing.

Finally, it should be mentioned that the assumption of a binary cost distribution is not straightforward. This distribution does not reflect the possibility that the expected cost of an unprofitable enrollee varies across risk adjustment groups. For example, young people whose expected costs are above the group average may have lower expected costs than elderly people for whom the same is true. This is likely the case because some types of health care expenditure are strongly correlated with age, even though total expenditure varies considerably within each age group. Therefore, the model results cannot be immediately generalized.

Nevertheless, the results still hold under more realistic assumptions. To show this, it is useful to consider a continuous cost distribution. In reality, the distribution of health care expenditure (even within given risk adjustment groups) is usually right-skewed, implying that the majority of the population has below-average costs. Moreover, the highest selection profits can still be obtained by sorting out the outliers within each cost group, and not by discriminating against particular groups. In the Appendix 3.B, it is shown that the intuition of the model generalizes to the case of a log-normal cost distribution.

3.4 Optimal Payment Scheme

3.4.1 General Assumptions

When looking for an optimal payment scheme, it must be specified which policies the regulator can implement. If the exact relationship between the insurer's cost

[22] See Myerson (1979).

reduction effort and realized health care costs is known, the first-best solution can theoretically be attained. This has been shown, in particular, by Barros (2003). The author suggests a payment scheme where the insurer obtains full reimbursement of the *difference* between individual health care expenditure and the average expenditure in the population (or in a subgroup with similar observable characteristics). This policy gives full incentives for cost efficiency and eliminates risk selection. However, the informational requirements of this approach are high, because it must be possible to assign total spending to specific diseases.

Here, we focus on a more realistic payment scheme involving partial cost reimbursement. In principle, cost sharing may be applied for all consumers or only for certain groups. An example for the first type of policies is outlier cost sharing, where a fixed percentage of individual costs above a certain threshold is reimbursed. This is particularly popular in practice. For example, in Germany, 60% of individual health care costs exceeding 21 051 Euro are reimbursed to the insurer.

The second group of policies involves cost sharing for a given number of individuals with the highest realized *or* predicted expenditure. In the latter case, the decision is based on individual health risk. In this spirit, van Barneveld et al. (1996) suggest that insurers may transfer a given percentage of their customers (typically, the worst risks in their portfolio) to a common pool. Assuming full cost reimbursement for this group, the authors show that substantial welfare gains could be attained even if only a small fraction of the insured (the simulations are based on a value of 5%) may be placed in the high-risk pool.

In the following, we explore the idea of cost sharing based on individual health risk in more detail. This allows the regulator to extract the insurer's private information, while minimizing the welfare loss which arises due to a reduction in cost efficiency. We assume that the regulator first commits to a set of contracts. Each contract specifies a fixed transfer t_j and the insurer's cost sharing rate α_j. Having chosen the effort levels e and a, the insurer must report his information on the consumer's risk type to the regulator. Upon a report of k_j, the consumer may be enrolled only under the contract (t_j, α_j). At the last stage, a fraction $1-\alpha_j$ of realized treatment costs is reimbursed.

The regulator's aim is to deter cream skimming. Thus, the insurer must be willing to enroll every risk type under the corresponding contract. We assume that

$\phi_h = \phi_l = 0$, implying that the insurer can dump all unprofitable consumers. This is not a restrictive assumption, and it has the advantage that the insurer's outside option becomes zero. As before, selection is not verifiable. In practice, the regulator cannot observe how many consumers seek enrollment, and also, some individuals may voluntarily switch to an outside alternative.

For simplicity, we limit the analysis to the information structure of Assumption 2. Here, the regulator offers only two contracts: the first one (t_h, α_h) is intended for the high-risk type (that is, for the case of full information), whereas the second contract, denoted by (t_x, α_x), will be chosen if the insurer remains uninformed. Moreover, we abstract from any statistical information. If the signal s is available, a pair of contracts can be offered for each subgroup, $s = 0, 1$. In this case, the probabilities p_h and p_l are to be replaced by conditional probabilities.

3.4.2 Insurer's Problem

Having accepted the contractual arrangement proposed by the regulator, the insurer chooses a cost reduction effort e and a level of information a to maximize his profit. Since the contracts have been designed in such a way that the insurer reveals his information on $j = h, x$ truthfully, and enrolls both groups of consumers, the profit function is given by:

$$\begin{aligned}\pi(a,e) = & p_h a\,[t_h - \alpha_h c_h(e)] + p_h(1-a)\,[t_x - \alpha_x c_h(e)] \\ & + p_l\,[t_x - \alpha_x c_l(e)] - g(e) - f(a)\end{aligned}$$

The first-order conditions are:

$$g'(e) = p_h a\, \alpha_h + (1 - p_h a)\, \alpha_x \tag{3.8}$$

$$f'(a) = p_h\,[t_h - \alpha_h c_h(e) - t_x + \alpha_x c_h(e)] \tag{3.9}$$

To ensure that the profit function is strictly concave, the determinant of the Hessian matrix must be positive, that is:

$$g''(e) f''(a) - p_h^2 (\alpha_h - \alpha_x)^2 > 0$$

This inequality will hold if the effort cost functions are sufficiently convex, in particular, if $g''(e)f''(a) \geq 1$.

Equation (3.8) implies that the effort e only depends on the *average* cost sharing rate. If this is smaller than one, cost efficiency will be distorted relative to the first-best level. Notice that it makes sense to restrict *both* rates between zero and one: If $\alpha_i < 0$, the insurer would have an incentive to spend additional resources on consumers of type i, apart from regular health care costs. In contrast, if $\alpha_i > 1$, the insurer could manipulate the payment system by absorbing the cost of type i personally.

According to equation (3.9), the marginal cost of information is equal to the increment in the insurer's rent for a high-risk consumer, when the true risk type is detected. Thus in an equilibrium with information acquisition, the difference in rents must be positive.

3.4.3 Regulator's Problem: Basic Results

At the contracting stage, the regulator chooses (t_h, α_h) and (t_x, α_x) to maximize social welfare. The welfare function is given by

$$\begin{aligned} W =& V + \pi(a,e) - (1+\omega_\pi)\left\{p_h a\left[t_h + (1-\alpha_h)\, c_h(e)\right] + \right. \\ & \left. p_h(1-a)\left[t_x + (1-\alpha_x)\, c_h(e)\right] + p_l\left[t_x + (1-\alpha_x)\, c_l(e)\right]\right\} \end{aligned} \tag{3.10}$$

where V denotes consumers' total benefit from enrollment. As this is constant, welfare maximization is equivalent to minimizing the total costs of health insurance coverage, subject to the participation and incentive constraints

$$t_h - \alpha_h c_h(e) - g(e) \geq 0 \tag{PC_h}$$

$$t_x - \alpha_x c_x(e) - g(e) \geq 0 \tag{PC_x}$$

$$t_h - \alpha_h c_h(e) \geq t_x - \alpha_x c_h(e) \tag{IC_h}$$

$$t_x - \alpha_x c_x(e) \geq t_h - \alpha_h c_x(e) \tag{IC_x}$$

$$\pi(a,e) \geq 0$$

and subject to the insurer's choice of a and e. The inequality in the last line is the ex ante participation constraint. It guarantees that the insurer is willing to operate under the proposed payment scheme, despite the investigation cost $f(a)$. In the following, we will ignore this constraint, assuming that it does not bind at the optimum. This is the case whenever $f(a)$ is not too high. The remaining (interim stage) participation constraints guarantee that the insurer makes at least zero profit with each risk type. Applying a standard argument, it can be shown that (PC_x) is redundant:

$$t_x - \alpha_x c_x(e) - g(e) \geq t_h - \alpha_h c_x(e) - g(e) > t_h - \alpha_h c_h(e) - g(e) \geq 0$$

If $a > 0$, the incentive (or truth-telling) constraint for the high-risk type cannot be binding, either: equation (3.9) shows that the insurer does not acquire any information if he needs to be forced to reveal it, that is, if (IC_h) holds with equality. In contrast, it can be shown that (PC_h) and (IC_x) are binding in equilibrium. This implies that the regulator adjusts the cost sharing rates, but not the transfer payments, to control the insurer's incentive for information acquisition. Then, t_h and t_x are chosen such that the insurer's informational rent is minimized.

Because the insurer's optimal levels of a and e are uniquely defined by the above first-order conditions, and since the profit function is assumed to be concave, the first-order approach can be applied. The rents for both consumer types can be inferred from the participation and incentive constraints.

Proposition 6 *In the optimal contracting framework, the insurer becomes informed with a positive probability in equilibrium. He receives zero rent when detecting a high-risk consumer and obtains a positive rent, on average, when uninformed. In the latter case, the rent for the high-risk type is negative, and that for the low-risk type is positive. Cost efficiency is distorted relative to the first-best solution, and the optimal cost sharing rates are characterized by* $0 \leq \alpha_h < \alpha_x \leq 1$.[23]

Although the insurer is given a positive rent when uninformed, information acquisition enables him to avoid losses with the high-risk type. This explains why it is not optimal to (completely) prevent the insurer from seeking private information. If this were the case, the incentive constraint (IC_h) would be binding, and the in-

[23] Proof: See Appendix 3.A.

surer would obtain zero rent for the high-risk type when uninformed (instead of a negative rent). Intuitively, this cannot be welfare maximizing.

It can be shown that the insurer's total rent amounts to

$$p_l\,\omega_\pi \alpha_h(k_h - k_l)$$

which is independent of a in equilibrium. The rent can be reduced by lowering the cost sharing rate for the high-risk type, at the expense of a reduction in cost efficiency. Since the cost sharing rate for the x-type does not directly influence the insurer's rent, it is optimal to set $\alpha_x > \alpha_h$ in order to limit the loss in efficiency. However, the standard result of "no distortion at the top", or $\alpha_x = 1$, does not apply. In fact, the degree to which the insurer can use information acquisition as a substitute for cost efficiency depends on the difference between the cost sharing rates:

$$\pi_{ae} = -p_h(\alpha_x - \alpha_h)$$

Thus, to prevent too much information acquisition, we will generally have $\alpha_x < 1$. As an exception, the corner solution may also occur.

3.4.4 Comparative Statics

Having derived the basic properties of the payment scheme, it remains to be shown how the optimal policy varies with the model parameters. It is convenient to focus on a setting where the effort cost functions are explicitly specified. Again, we consider the quadratic case:

$$g(e) = \frac{r_e e^2}{2}; \qquad f(a) = \frac{r_a a^2}{2}$$

The parameters r_a and r_e reflect the level of the insurer's effort costs. Smaller values of r_e imply that treatment costs can be reduced at a relatively low expenditure of resources. This may be the case if the insurer can offer managed care contracts, as opposed to traditional health insurance. Also, cost savings may be more easily realized for some medical conditions than for others. For example, many insurers have implemented disease management programs which are at least partly aimed at reducing the costs of certain chronic diseases (e.g., diabetes, coronary heart disease). Arguably, this corresponds to a setting where r_e is relatively low. The cost of information acquisition r_a may also depend on the organizational framework. For instance, an insurer who offers supplementary health insurance in addition to the basic benefit package, or who operates a wide network of insurance agents, can identify high-risk consumers at a relatively low cost.

Proposition 7 states that the optimal cost reduction effort depends negatively on the parameter r_e. This is intuitive: if the marginal effort cost declines, the insurer will exert more effort under a given payment scheme. In equilibrium, the cost sharing rates α_x and α_h are also raised as r_e falls. This gives the insurer an even stronger incentive for cost efficiency, but entails a welfare loss in the form of a higher rent. Here, the gain from more effective cost reduction outweighs the loss. Moreover, an increase in the insurer's rent as such has a negative effect on the optimal effort level.[24]

Proposition 7 *The optimal cost reduction effort is decreasing in the level of the insurer's rent $p_l\,\omega_\pi(k_h - k_l)$ and in the effort cost parameter r_e.*

Since the rent is increasing in the proportion of low risks, cost efficiency must be decreasing in this parameter. Clearly, increases in the term $k_h - k_l$, which determines the insurer's incentive for risk selection, and in the weight on insurer rents have a similar effect.

The next result concerns the optimal level of information. Here, changes in the investigation cost parameter r_a and in the cost difference $k_h - k_l$ only have a second-order effect. In contrast, an increase in the shadow price ω_π has a positive effect on information acquisition. The intuition for this result is the following. As mentioned above, it is costly to prevent the insurer from seeking private information, and this cost is increasing in ω_π. By implementing a higher level of a, the insurer's loss from an undetected high-risk consumer increases, although he is more likely to avoid this loss (and obtain zero rent instead). As the effort cost function $f(a)$ is convex, it can be shown that the total effect on social welfare is positive. Finally, the optimal level of a is inversely related to the proportion of high-risk consumers. This is because the optimal number of high risks who are detected $(p_h a)$ is constant in the present framework. Proposition 8 summarizes.

[24] This result can be generalized to all effort cost functions where $g'''(e) \geq 0$.

Proposition 8 *The optimal level of information is decreasing in the proportion of high-risk consumers p_h and increasing in the weight on insurer rents ω_π.*

Proposition 9 describes the effects of the model parameters on the optimal payment scheme. Apart from the effort cost parameter r_e, the optimal cost sharing rates also depend on the level of informational costs. As the levels of information and cost reduction effort are independent of r_a, the cost sharing rates must be adapted such that the insurer's choices remain unchanged. This implies more cost reimbursement for the h-type and stronger incentives for efficiency if the insurer remains uninformed. If r_a is relatively high, a corner solution may arise where $\alpha_x = 1$ or $\alpha_h = 0$.

An increase in the insurer's rent via the term $\omega_\pi(k_h - k_l)$ has an opposite effect, in the sense that the difference between the cost sharing rates $(\alpha_x - \alpha_h)$ is reduced. On the other hand, an increase in the incentive for selection, as represented by the term $k_h - k_l$, has a negative effect on the optimal level of cost efficiency, and thus on α_x. Moreover, an increase in the shadow price ω_π leads to a reduction in α_h, implying a lower level of cost efficiency and a higher level of information. The remaining effects are ambiguous.

Proposition 9 *The optimal cost sharing rates depend on the model parameters as follows:*
(i) α_x *is decreasing in* r_e*, increasing in* r_a*, and decreasing in* $k_h - k_l$*.*
(ii) α_h *is decreasing in* r_e*,* r_a *and* ω_π*.*
(iii) $\alpha_x - \alpha_h$ *is decreasing in* $k_h - k_l$ *and in* ω_π*.*

To summarize, risk selection can be prevented by giving the insurer a rent for the group of consumers that has lower predicted costs. There is a trade-off between the size of the rent and cost efficiency, implying that the equilibrium effort for cost reduction falls below the first-best level. The possibility of information acquisition improves this trade-off, because it allows to reduce the insurer's rent. Since the insurer perceives cost efficiency and information acquisition as substitutes, however, the level of information should not become too high. Generally, cost reimbursement becomes more attractive if the incentive for risk selection increases, or if the welfare loss due to insurer rents becomes more important.

3.4.5 Discussion

It has been shown that cost sharing based on (the insurer's information on) expected health care costs maximizes social welfare in the model framework. The optimal payment scheme is more complex than the policy proposed by van Barneveld et al. (1996). On the one hand, full cost reimbursement for high-risk consumers is generally not desirable. On the other hand, the optimal payment scheme may involve cost sharing also for other risk types. This could be implemented by offering different reimbursement rates (or risk-sharing pools) for different percentiles of the expected cost distribution.

An important implication is that cost sharing should be combined with statistical information on individual risk types.[25] Ideally, the regulator should offer a pair of contracts for each risk adjustment group ($s = 0, 1$). Such a payment scheme would become quite complex if the number of cost groups increases. In practice, a combination between conventional risk adjustment and cost sharing for individuals with relatively high expected costs seems more realistic.

As mentioned, the model is closely related to the contribution by Sappington and Lewis (1999). In contrast to the present model, the authors do not consider information acquisition as a probabilistic choice. Instead, the insurer can become fully informed after incurring a fixed cost. If this cost is high enough, it is optimal for the regulator to deter information acquisition. This assumption, however, may not be very realistic because part of the insurer's private information may be relatively easy to obtain.

Another difference concerns the role of statistical information. Sappington and Lewis show that it may not be optimal to make the payment scheme conditional on a stochastic signal, because deterring information acquisition may become more expensive in this case. Although their argument goes in a similar direction as that of Section 3.3, this result cannot be confirmed within the optimal contracting framework. Indeed, Sappington and Lewis show that including statistical information improves upon the optimal payment scheme in an equilibrium *with* information acquisition. This generally applies to the present model as well.[26]

[25] See the discussion below.

[26] A sufficient but not necessary condition here is that the maximized welfare function be concave in p_l.

Finally, it should be mentioned that the model can be amended to capture also the information structure of Assumption 1. In this framework, the regulator offers three contracts: one for high-risk and low-risk consumers, respectively, and one for the case where the insurer is uninformed. Consequently, the number of constraints increases. It can be easily shown that only the participation constraint for the high-risk type is binding, whereas the other participation constraints are redundant. In addition, two incentive constraints are binding: As before, the insurer must not be given an incentive to pretend high costs when he is indeed uninformed. He must also be prevented from announcing average costs when he has identified a low-risk consumer.[27] This implies that the rent for a low-risk consumer exceeds that of the average type. Clearly, the total welfare loss is larger than in the above model.[28]

Under this extension, information acquisition would become less desirable from a social perspective. However, the basic properties of the model would not change dramatically. In particular, the cost sharing rate must still be decreasing in the consumer's health risk, such that $\alpha_h < \alpha_x \leq \alpha_l$. As α_l does not affect the decision on information acquisition, it is optimal to set $\alpha_l = 1$. Thus there is no distortion at the top.

3.5 Conclusion

Although it is often mentioned that existing risk adjustment schemes are imperfect, it is also widely believed that they perform at least better than a system without risk adjustment. Assuming that risk selection entails an informational cost for the insurer, it has been shown that this may not be the case. The results of Section 3.3 particularly strengthen the argument against simple compensations schemes, for example, based only on age and sex of the insured.

Of course, the model assumptions have been chosen in order to keep the model as simple and tractable as possible. Some qualifications must be made. An aspect which has not been taken into account is that part of the insurer's private information

[27] In other words, only the downward incentive constraints for neighboring types must be taken into account.

[28] It can be shown that the rent amounts to $\omega_\pi(k_k - k_l)[p_l\alpha_h + p_l p_h a(\alpha_x - \alpha_h)]$, which directly depends on a. Thus the interaction between cost efficiency and information acquisition becomes more complex.

may be freely observable. This would be an argument in favor of imperfect risk adjustment. In practice, insurers are also willing to enroll applicants who generate small expected losses; risk adjustment normally reduces the number of individuals who generate substantial profits and losses. Moreover, even if variables such as age and sex are only weakly correlated with individual health care costs, they may be perfectly correlated with some types of expenditure (e.g., maternity care). If these factors are taken into account, even a simple risk adjustment scheme will less likely be strictly inferior to the reference case. However, the general direction of the results will remain the same. Most notably, the benefit of statistical risk adjustment is less obvious than often assumed.

The model also describes a development which may take place in the health insurance market over time. In order to "beat" the risk adjustment system, insurers have a strong incentive to develop better statistical methods for predicting their potential enrollees' costs. There is indeed some evidence for an "information race". For instance, Beck et al. (2006) present a regression model which predicts 46-48% of the annual health care costs of the sample population, about 250000 persons enrolled with a Swiss health insurer in 2000. This seems to reflect the level of information that can be obtained by insurers quite well. In contrast, the older literature, including Newhouse et al. (1989) and van Vliet (1992), suggested that only 20-25% of the variation in individual expenditure could be predicted at all.

Section 3.4 has shown that cost sharing based on individual health risk is optimal to prevent cream skimming. In practice, cost reimbursement and statistical risk adjustment are often considered as substitutes. For example, in the Netherlands, the introduction of an improved risk adjustment formula in 2002 enabled the government to raise the threshold value for outlier cost sharing.[29] It should be analyzed in more detail how different tools for reducing selection can best be combined.

Unlike cost reimbursement, conventional risk adjustment has the advantage that, in principle, it does not distort incentives for cost efficiency. Risk adjustment based on medical information, however, leaves room for manipulation, as there is an incentive to "upcode" diagnoses in order to obtain higher payments. In Germany, upcoding seems to be an important problem[30] since a morbidity-based risk adjustment

[29] See van de Ven and Schut (2007).

[30] In the United States, a reform bill has recently been proposed which would require Medicare payments to be adjusted for upcoding problems. See Angeles and Park (2009).

formula has been introduced in 2009. The optimal contracting approach avoids this problem and should therefore be given more consideration in practice.

Although risk selection does not currently play an important role in the German social health insurance market, future reforms might give insurers more discretion over the form of insurance contracts which can be offered. This would foster competition between insurers, but would increase the scope for selection. In this context, an adequate payment scheme could provide the foundation for successful reform.[31]

3.A Proofs

Preliminaries

Throughout the analysis, we use the following transformations:

$$\begin{aligned}
\bar{k}-k_h &= p_h k_h + p_l k_l - k_h = -p_l(k_h-k_l) \\
\bar{k}-k_l &= p_h k_h + p_l k_l - k_l = p_h(k_h-k_l) \\
k_s-k_h &= p_{h|s} k_h + p_{l|s} k_l - k_h = -p_{l|s}(k_h-k_l) \\
k_s-k_l &= p_{h|s} k_h + p_{l|s} k_l - k_l = p_{h|s}(k_h-k_l)
\end{aligned}$$

Enrollment Decision

Here, we derive the inequalities (3.1) and (3.2). Given the signal s, the insurer encourages enrollment if:

$$\begin{aligned}
p_{h|s}(\bar{k}-k_h)+p_{l|s}(\bar{k}-k_l) &\geq p_{h|s}\phi_h(\bar{k}-k_h)+p_{l|s}\phi_l(\bar{k}-k_l) \\
-p_{h|s}p_l(k_h-k_l)+p_h p_{l|s}(k_h-k_l) &\geq -p_{h|s}p_l\phi_h(k_h-k_l)+p_h p_{l|s}\phi_l(k_h-k_l) \\
p_h p_l \frac{p_{s|l}}{p_s}(1-\phi_l)(k_h-k_l) &\geq p_h p_l \frac{p_{s|h}}{p_s}(1-\phi_h)(k_h-k_l) \\
p_{s|l}(1-\phi_l) &\geq p_{s|h}(1-\phi_h)
\end{aligned}$$

[31] The results by Nuscheler and Knaus (2005) strengthen this argument. They show that some insurers can substantially benefit from imperfect risk adjustment in combination with a favorable risk structure, even if they do not actively practice selection. This is due to historical reasons, and to the negative correlation between health status and switching costs.

Information Acquisition

For convenience, we denote the insurer's objective function for each case. In the absence of risk adjustment, and conditional on observing $s = 0$, the expected profit amounts to:

$$\begin{aligned} E[\pi^N|0] =& a_0^N \left[p_{h|0}\,\phi_h(\bar{k}-k_h) + p_{l|0}(\bar{k}-k_l)\right] + \\ & (1-a_0^N)\left[p_{h|0}\,(\bar{k}-k_h) + p_{l|0}\,(\bar{k}-k_l)\right] - f(a_0^N) \end{aligned}$$

If $s = 1$ is observed, the insurer maximizes:

$$\begin{aligned} E[\pi^N|1] =& a_1^N \left[p_{h|1}\,\phi_h(\bar{k}-k_h) + p_{l|1}(\bar{k}-k_l)\right] + \\ & (1-a_1^N)\left[p_{h|1}\,\phi_h(\bar{k}-k_h) + p_{l|1}\,\phi_l(\bar{k}-k_l)\right] - f(a_1^N) \end{aligned}$$

In the *RA*-system, the expected profit, conditional on s, is given by:

$$E[\pi^{RA}|s] = a_s^{RA}\left[p_{h|s}\,\phi_h(k_s-k_h) + p_{l|s}(k_s-k_l)\right] - f(a_s^{RA})$$

Taking the derivative and applying the above transformations, one obtains the first-order conditions (3.3), (3.4) and (3.5).

Proof of Proposition 6

Using the constraints (PC_h) and (IC_x) to eliminate the transfers t_h and t_x, and applying the first-order approach, the regulator's problem becomes:

$$\begin{aligned} \max_{\alpha_h,\alpha_x,a,e} \; L =& V-(1+\omega_\pi)[\bar{k}+e-g(e)] - f(a) - p_l\,\omega_\pi\alpha_h(k_h-k_l) \\ & + \lambda\left\{p_h a\,\alpha_h + (1-p_h a)\,\alpha_x - g'(e)\right\} \\ & + \mu\left\{p_h(\alpha_x-\alpha_h)(k_h-k_x) - f'(a)\right\} \end{aligned} \tag{3.11}$$

The first-order conditions are given by:

$$\frac{\partial L}{\partial \alpha_h} = -p_l\,\omega_\pi(k_h-k_l) + \lambda\,p_h a - \mu\frac{p_h p_l(k_h-k_l)}{1-p_h a} \leq 0 \tag{3.12}$$

Moreover:

$$\frac{\partial L}{\partial \alpha_x} = \lambda(1-p_h a) + \mu \frac{p_h p_l (k_h - k_l)}{1-p_h a} \geq 0 \tag{3.13}$$

$$\frac{\partial L}{\partial a} = -f'(a) - \lambda p_h(\alpha_x - \alpha_h) + \mu p_h \frac{p_h p_l (k_h - k_l)}{(1-p_h a)^2}(\alpha_x - \alpha_h) - \mu f''(a) = 0 \tag{3.14}$$

$$\frac{\partial L}{\partial e} = (1+\omega_\pi)[1-g'(e)] - \lambda g''(e) = 0 \tag{3.15}$$

The "complementary slackness" conditions require that:

$$\frac{\partial L}{\partial \alpha_h}\alpha_h = 0; \qquad \frac{\partial L}{\partial \alpha_x}(1-\alpha_x) = 0$$

We show that there is information acquisition in equilibrium, or $a > 0$. Formally, the optimization problem for the case *without* information acquisition is a special case of problem (3.11), where $a = 0$ and $\alpha_x = \alpha_h$. From equation (3.14), we can infer that the marginal benefit of information is positive at this point:

$$\left.\frac{\partial L}{\partial a}\right|_{a=0} = -f'(0) - \mu f''(0) > 0$$

This inequality holds because we assumed $f'(0) = 0$ and because the shadow price associated with the first-order condition for the choice of a must be negative.

Proof of Proposition 7

We focus on the case of an interior solution. Here, combining equations (3.12) and (3.13) yields:

$$\lambda = p_l\, \omega_\pi (k_h - k_l)$$

$$\mu = -\frac{\omega_\pi (1-p_h a)^2}{p_h}$$

The comparative statics of the effort level e can be analyzed more generally. Applying the implicit function theorem to equation (3.15) yields:

$$\frac{\partial e}{\partial p_l (k_h - k_l)} = -\frac{-g''(e)}{-(1+\omega_\pi)g''(e) - \lambda g'''(e)}$$

This holds at least if $g'''(e) \geq 0$. Similarly, we have:

$$\frac{\partial e}{\partial \omega_\pi} = -\frac{1 - g'(e) - p_l(k_h - k_l)g''(e)}{-(1+\omega_\pi)g''(e) - \lambda g'''(e)}$$

Using equation (3.15), the numerator can be expressed as $-[1-g'(e)]/\omega_\pi$ which must be negative in equilibrium. Thus, $g'''(e) \geq 0$ is still a sufficient condition for this derivative to be negative. In the quadratic case, we have:

$$e = \frac{1}{r_e} - \frac{\omega_\pi}{1+\omega_\pi} p_l(k_h - k_l)$$

This is also decreasing in ω_π.

Proof of Proposition 8

Inserting the above expressions for λ and π into equation (3.14), multiplying by p_h and rearranging, we obtain:

$$2p_h^2 p_l\, \omega_\pi(\alpha_x - \alpha_h)(k_h - k_l) = \omega_\pi(1 - p_h a)^2 f''(a) - p_h f'(a) \tag{3.16}$$

The insurer's first-order condition can be expressed as:

$$p_h p_l(\alpha_x - \alpha_h)(k_h - k_l) = (1 - p_h a) f'(a) \tag{3.17}$$

In the quadratic case, equations (3.16) and (3.17) take the following form:

$$2p_h^2 p_l\, \omega_\pi(\alpha_x - \alpha_h)(k_h - k_l) = \omega_\pi(1 - 2p_h a + p_h^2 a^2)\, r_a - p_h a\, r_a$$

$$p_h p_l(\alpha_x - \alpha_h)(k_h - k_l) = (a - p_h a^2) r_a$$

Multiplying the second equation by $p_h \omega_\pi$ and adding up:

$$3p_h^2 p_l\, \omega_\pi(\alpha_x - \alpha_h)(k_h - k_l) = (1 - 2p_h a) r_a$$

Rearranging yields:

$$p_h p_l(\alpha_x - \alpha_h)(k_h - k_l) = \frac{\omega_\pi - p_h a(1+\omega_\pi)}{3p_h\omega_\pi} r_a$$

After inserting this into equation (3.17), we can solve for a:

$$a = \frac{1+4\omega_\pi - \sqrt{4\omega_\pi^2 + 8\omega_\pi + 1}}{6p_h\omega_\pi}$$

We show that a is increasing in ω_π. Multiplying by $6p_h$ and differentiating:

$$-\frac{1}{\omega_\pi^2}\left(1 - \sqrt{4\omega_\pi^2 + 8\omega_\pi + 1}\right) - \frac{1}{\omega_\pi}\frac{4\omega_\pi + 4}{\sqrt{4\omega_\pi^2 + 8\omega_\pi + 1}} > 0$$

$$-\left(\sqrt{4\omega_\pi^2 + 8\omega_\pi + 1} - (4\omega_\pi^2 + 8\omega_\pi + 1)\right) - \omega_\pi(4\omega_\pi + 4) > 0$$

$$\sqrt{4\omega_\pi^2 + 8\omega_\pi + 1} < 4\omega_\pi + 1$$

This holds for all $\omega_\pi > 0$. Moreover, it can be shown that the proportion of high risks who are detected ($p_h a$) tends to $\frac{1}{3}$ as ω_π goes to infinity. Thus, there is always an interior solution if $p_h > \frac{1}{3}$.

Proof of Proposition 9

The insurer's first-order condition can be solved for:

$$\alpha_x - \alpha_h = \frac{2\omega_\pi^2 - 5\omega_\pi - 1 + (1+\omega_\pi)\sqrt{1 + 4\omega_\pi^2 + 8\omega_\pi}}{18p_h^2 p_l\,\omega_\pi^2(k_h - k_l)} r_a$$

We show that this is increasing in ω_π. Multiplying by $18p_h^2 p_l(k_h - k_l)/r_a$ and differentiating yields:

$$\frac{5}{\omega_\pi^2} + \frac{2}{\omega_\pi^3} - \left(\frac{2}{\omega_\pi^3} + \frac{1}{\omega_\pi^2}\right)\sqrt{4\omega_\pi^2 + 8\omega_\pi + 1} + \left(\frac{1}{\omega_\pi^2} + \frac{1}{\omega_\pi}\right)\frac{4\omega_\pi + 4}{\sqrt{\cdots}} > 0$$

$$(5\omega_\pi + 2)\sqrt{\cdots} - (2+\omega_\pi)\left(4\omega_\pi^2 + 8\omega_\pi + 1\right) + (\omega_\pi + \omega_\pi^2)(4\omega_\pi + 4) > 0$$

Rearranging and taking the square, we obtain

$$
\begin{aligned}
(5\omega_\pi+2)^2\left(4\omega_\pi^2+8\omega_\pi+1\right) &> \left(8\omega_\pi^2+13\omega_\pi+2\right)^2 \\
100\omega_\pi^4+280\omega_\pi^3+201\omega_\pi^2+52\omega_\pi+4 &> 64\omega_\pi^4+208\omega_\pi^3+201\omega_\pi^2+52\omega_\pi+4 \\
36\,\omega_\pi^3\,(\omega_\pi+2) &> 0
\end{aligned}
$$

which must be true.

The optimal level of cost reimbursement is related to the cost reduction effort e. Equation (3.15) and the insurer's first-order condition take the form:

$$
\begin{aligned}
r_e\,e &= 1-\frac{\omega_\pi}{1+\omega_\pi}\,p_l\,r_e(k_h-k_l) \\
r_e\,e &= p_h a\,\alpha_h+(1-p_h a)\,\alpha_x
\end{aligned}
$$

This can be expressed as:

$$
\begin{aligned}
\alpha_h &= 1-\frac{\omega_\pi}{1+\omega_\pi}\,p_l\,r_e(k_h-k_l)-(1-p_h a)(\alpha_x-\alpha_h) \\
\alpha_x &= 1-\frac{\omega_\pi}{1+\omega_\pi}\,p_l\,\omega_\pi r_e(k_h-k_l)+p_h a(\alpha_x-\alpha_h)
\end{aligned}
$$

The signs of the derivatives $\partial\alpha_i/\partial r_e$, $\partial\alpha_i/\partial r_a$ and $\partial\alpha_x/\partial(k_h-k_l)$ can be inferred when $\alpha_x-\alpha_h$ is replaced by the above expression. To prove that $\partial\alpha_h/\partial\omega_\pi<0$, we show that the term $(1-p_h a)(\alpha_x-\alpha_h)$ is increasing in ω_π. This can be written as:

$$
\frac{1}{54p_h^2p_l(k_h-k_l)}\left[4+\frac{6}{\omega_\pi^2}+\frac{1}{\omega_\pi^3}+\left(\frac{2}{\omega_\pi}-\frac{2}{\omega_\pi^2}-\frac{1}{\omega_\pi^3}\right)\sqrt{\cdots}\right]
$$

The derivative of the second factor is given by:

$$
-\frac{12}{\omega_\pi^3}-\frac{3}{\omega_\pi^4}+\left(-\frac{2}{\omega_\pi^2}+\frac{4}{\omega_\pi^3}+\frac{3}{\omega_\pi^4}\right)\sqrt{\cdots}+\left(\frac{2}{\omega_\pi}-\frac{2}{\omega_\pi^2}-\frac{1}{\omega_\pi^3}\right)\frac{4\omega_\pi+4}{\sqrt{\cdots}}
$$

After multiplying by $\sqrt{\cdot}\,\omega_\pi^4$, we find that this is positive if:

$$
\begin{aligned}
(4\omega_\pi^2+8\omega_\pi+1)(-2\omega_\pi^2+4\omega_\pi+3)+(2\omega_\pi^3-2\omega_\pi^2-2\omega_\pi)(4\omega_\pi+4)& \\
>(12\omega_\pi+3)\sqrt{\cdots}&
\end{aligned}
$$

This can be rearranged to

$$
\begin{aligned}
(10\omega_\pi^2+24\omega_\pi+3)^2 &> (4\omega_\pi+1)^2(4\omega_\pi^2+8\omega_\pi+1)\\
100\omega_\pi^4+160\omega_\pi^3+84\omega_\pi^2+16\omega_\pi+1 &> 64\omega_\pi^4+160\omega_\pi^3+84\omega_\pi^2+16\omega_\pi+1\\
100 &> 64
\end{aligned}
$$

which completes the proof.

3.B The Continuous Case

In the following, we analyze the effects of statistical risk adjustment under the more realistic assumption of a continuous cost distribution. The aim is to show that the results of Section 3.3 are not specific to the binary distribution considered above. In addition, the analysis shows how the model could be applied to concrete health insurance data. We assume that the calculation of the transfer payments is based on a regression model. As before, the insurer may look for private information to make a more accurate cost prediction. This situation has also been analyzed by Newhouse et al. (1989) and van Barneveld et al. (2000), whose model framework is applied to the case of endogenous information.

3.B.1 The Model

Suppose that both the regulator and the insurer can observe a vector of consumer characteristics X_1, that may be used in the risk adjustment formula. As before, the insurer can exert an effort to acquire some private information. With probability a, he can observe several additional variables which are correlated with individual health risk. These are given by the vector X_2. For simplicity, we assume that the effort a is chosen independently from observable consumer characteristics. This can be justified if the insurer uses a standardized procedure to screen applicants' health risks. In a wider sense, the function $f(a)$ may also represent the cost of developing better statistical methods for predicting individual expenditure.

To account for the fact health care costs usually have a right-skewed distribution, we consider the case of a log-normal distribution. Total costs are denoted by C. We do not explicitly model the insurer's cost reduction effort. However, C can be interpreted to represent the efficient cost level, resulting from a socially optimal choice of e. Based on the available information (either X_1 or X_1 and X_2), the following cost predictions are obtained:

$$\log C = X_1\beta_1 + \varepsilon_1$$
$$\log C = X_1\beta_1 + X_2\beta_2 + \varepsilon_2$$

The error terms ε_1 and ε_2 are normally distributed with mean zero. The vectors X_1 and X_2 are assumed to be orthogonal, implying that they are also uncorrelated. Although this may be too strong an assumption in reality, it is a useful generalization. Moreover, we assume that $X_1\beta_1$ and $X_2\beta_2$ have means μ_1 and μ_2, and standard deviations σ_1 and σ_2, respectively. The total variance is given by $\sigma^2 = \sigma_1^2 + \sigma_2^2 + \sigma_3^2$, where σ_3^2 denotes the variance of the error term ε_2. Thus, σ_1^2 represents the part of the variation in health care costs that can be predicted by the regulator, σ_2^2 represents the additional part that may be predicted by the insurer, and σ_3^2 is the unpredictable part.

Based on the properties of the log-normal distribution, the unconditional expectation of health care costs is given by:

$$E(C) = e^{\mu_1+\mu_2+\frac{1}{2}\sigma^2} \tag{3.18}$$

If there is no risk adjustment, the insurer receives a transfer payment based on (3.18) for each enrolled consumer. For an individual with characteristics X_1 and X_2, the risk-adjusted capitation payment and the insurer's cost prediction (if better informed) are given by equations (3.19) and (3.20), respectively.

$$E(C|X_1) = e^{X_1\beta_1+\mu_2+\frac{1}{2}(\sigma_2^2+\sigma_3^2)} \tag{3.19}$$
$$E(C|X_1,X_2) = e^{X_1\beta_1+X_2\beta_2+\frac{1}{2}\sigma_3^2} \tag{3.20}$$

In the *RA* system, the insurer expects an individual consumer to be profitable if $X_2\beta_2 < \mu_2 + \frac{1}{2}\sigma_2^2$, or:

$$\frac{X_2\beta_2 - \mu_2}{\sigma_2} < \frac{\sigma_2}{2}$$

The term on the left-hand side follows a standard normal distribution. Its cumulative distribution function is denoted by Φ. For simplicity, we assume that risk selection is always possible, or $\phi_i = 0$. Given the insurer can observe X_2, the probability that a consumer is rejected equals $1 - \Phi(\sigma_2/2)$.

In the case without risk adjustment, the probability of *enrollment* also depends on the insurer's level of information. It is given by $\Phi(\sigma_1/2)$ if only X_1 is observable, and by

$$\Phi\left(\sqrt{\sigma_1^2 + \sigma_2^2}/2\right)$$

if X_2 can also be observed. The second expression results because the term $X_1\beta_1 + X_2\beta_2$ is normally distributed with mean $\mu_1 + \mu_2$ and variance $\sigma_1^2 + \sigma_2^2$.

3.B.2 Results

Again, we want to answer the question whether risk adjustment based on a given set of variables X_1 is superior to a system without risk adjustment. The following statement, concerning the insurer's level of information, confirms the result of the binary case.

Remark 1 *In the continuous model, with the selection probability ϕ being equal for all risk types, the insurer becomes informed with a higher probability in the RA-system than in the N-system.*

To prove this, we have to determine the insurer's potential profit from risk selection. For instance, in the *RA*-system, and given the information X_2, the average expenditure for an enrolled consumer amounts to:

$$\begin{aligned}
&E\left[\exp\{X_1\beta_1 + X_2\beta_2 + \sigma_3^2/2\} \mid (X_2\beta_2 - \mu_2)/\sigma_2 < \sigma_2/2\right] \\
&= \exp\{\mu_1 + (\sigma_1^2 + \sigma_3^2)/2\}\, E\left[\exp\{X_2\beta_2\} \mid (X_2\beta_2 - \mu_2)/\sigma_2 < \sigma_2/2\right] \\
&= \exp\{\mu_1 + (\sigma_1^2 + \sigma_3^2)/2\} \exp\{\mu_2 + \sigma_2^2/2\} \frac{1 - \Phi(\sigma_2/2)}{\Phi(\sigma_2/2)} \\
&= \frac{1 - \Phi(\sigma_2/2)}{\Phi(\sigma_2/2)} E(C)
\end{aligned}$$

This follows directly from the properties of the log-normal distribution. In contrast, the average transfer payment is unaffected by the insurer's selection activities:

$$E\left[\exp\{X_1\beta_1 + \mu_2 + (\sigma_2^2 + \sigma_3^2)/2\} | (X_2\beta_2 - \mu_2)/\sigma_2 < \sigma_2/2\right] = E(C)$$

This equation is a consequence of the orthogonality assumption. Of course, in the absence of private information, the insurer makes zero profit. The first-order condition for the choice of a^{RA} is given by:

$$f'(a^{RA}) = E(C)\left[2\Phi(\sigma_2/2) - 1\right] \tag{3.21}$$

In the reference case without risk adjustment, the first-order condition can be derived in a similar way:

$$f'(a^N) = E(C)\left\{\left[2\Phi\left(\sqrt{\sigma_1^2 + \sigma_2^2}/2\right) - 1\right] - \left[2\Phi(\sigma_1/2) - 1\right]\right\} \tag{3.22}$$

The marginal benefit of information corresponds to the increment in the insurer's selection profit. Intuitively, this is smaller than in the *RA*-case because the insurer can make a positive profit even without observing X_2. Formally, convexity of the effort cost function implies that $a^{RA} \geq a^N$ if:

$$\Phi(\sigma_1/2) + \Phi(\sigma_2/2) \geq \Phi\left(\sqrt{\sigma_1^2 + \sigma_2^2}/2\right) + \underbrace{\Phi(0)}_{1/2}$$

We can use the fact that $\sqrt{\sigma_1^2 + \sigma_2^2} \leq \sigma_1 + \sigma_2$. Thus it is sufficient to show that:

$$\Phi(\sigma_1/2) + \Phi(\sigma_2/2) \geq \Phi\left[(\sigma_1 + \sigma_2)/2\right] + \Phi(0)$$

For convenience, we denote $x = \sigma_1/2$ and $y = \sigma_2/2$. Now, it can be demonstrated for all $x, y \geq 0$ that:

$$\Phi(x) + \Phi(y) \geq \Phi(x+y) + \Phi(0)$$

This can be written out as:

$$\int_{-\infty}^{x} \frac{e^{-\frac{1}{2}u^2}}{\sqrt{2\pi}} du + \int_{-\infty}^{y} \frac{e^{-\frac{1}{2}u^2}}{\sqrt{2\pi}} du \geq \int_{-\infty}^{x+y} \frac{e^{-\frac{1}{2}u^2}}{\sqrt{2\pi}} du + \int_{-\infty}^{0} \frac{e^{-\frac{1}{2}u^2}}{\sqrt{2\pi}} du$$

Rearranging the integral terms, this reduces to:

$$\int_0^y \frac{e^{-\frac{1}{2}u^2}}{\sqrt{2\pi}} du \geq \int_x^{x+y} \frac{e^{-\frac{1}{2}u^2}}{\sqrt{2\pi}} du$$

This must be true because the density function $\frac{1}{\sqrt{2\pi}} e^{-\frac{1}{2}u^2}$ is strictly decreasing in $u > 0$, and holds with equality if $x = 0$ or $y = 0$.

Moreover, a comparison of the shares of enrolled consumers yields ambiguous results:

Remark 2 *The share of individuals that the insurer would like to reject is higher in the RA-system than in the N-system if:*

$$a^{RA}\left[1-\Phi(\sigma_2/2)\right] > a^N\left[1-\Phi\left(\sqrt{\sigma_1^2+\sigma_2^2}/2\right)\right] + (1-a^N)\left[1-\Phi(\sigma_1/2)\right]$$

This inequality certainly holds if $a_N = 1$, such that the second term of the right-hand side vanishes. Generally, if a^N is relatively high, the level of selection may be higher under risk adjustment than in the reference case.

Finally, we can also draw some conclusions regarding the insurer's potential profit from cream skimming. Remark 3 implies that risk adjustment is less attractive if the degree of asymmetric information, measured by σ_2, is high.

Remark 3 *The insurer's selection profit may be higher in the RA-system than in the N-system. A necessary but not sufficient condition for this case to occur is $\sigma_2 > \sigma_1$.*

From equation (3.21), we can infer that risk adjustment is superior if the term σ_2^2, representing the extent of the insurer's private information, is relatively small. Thus a sufficiently accurate risk adjustment scheme is always desirable.

Chapter 4

Watchfully Waiting: Medical Intervention as an Optimal Investment Decision

4.1 Introduction

"Watchfully waiting" involves monitoring a patient's health state over time and deciding whether or not to undertake a medical intervention - an operation, course of treatment or some other medical procedure. This process is characterized by the three essential properties of an investment decision: the existence of uncertainty, in this case concerning the development of the patient's health state and, possibly, the outcome of medical intervention; irreversibility, in the sense that the results of the intervention may be impossible or extremely costly to reverse; and flexibility of timing, implying that a key aspect of the decision is exactly when to make the intervention. At each point in time, there is the possibility of making the intervention or of postponing it and observing how the patient's health state evolves. Recent developments in the theory of investment under uncertainty[1] have greatly increased our understanding of how such decisions should be taken, and this paper is concerned with the application of this theory to the watching and waiting process.

---

[1] Seminal contributions involve McDonald and Siegel (1986), Pindyck (1988) and Dixit (1989). Dixit and Pindyck (1994) give a thorough review of the techniques and literature.

A key insight of the theory of investment under uncertainty, also referred to as the "real options" approach, concerns the option value of waiting. A standard proposition of traditional investment theory is that an investment should be undertaken if (when) the present value of its benefits exceeds the present value of its costs. This, however, ignores the possibility that information about the inherently uncertain costs and benefits may be revealed over time, and so it may pay to postpone the investment beyond the break-even point in order to collect more information. That is, the option to wait has a positive value, while making the investment, in the present case carrying out the medical intervention, extinguishes this option and sacrifices its value. Thus the net present value may have to be (substantially) greater than zero to trigger investment.

In this paper, we present a formal model of the watchfully waiting process and derive decision rules for switching to direct intervention. This amounts to an optimal stopping problem: the patient's health state is assumed to follow a stochastic process, and medical intervention terminates this process and restores the patient's health. A distinctive feature of our model is the possibility that the patient's condition may improve spontaneously. As discussed below, this is an important motivation for the watchfully waiting strategy. Formally, we assume that the patient's health state may reach the absorbing state of full health at some point in time. Thus, the benefit of waiting involves the possibility of spontaneous recovery as well as the value of the option to perform the intervention at a later point in time.

Our central result concerns the effect of uncertainty on the decision to treat the patient. If the patient's health state has a central tendency to deteriorate (net of the discount rate), a higher degree of variability in the development of the disease will make waiting more attractive, in the sense that direct intervention will be optimal for a smaller range of health states. This corresponds to the standard result of the real options literature. On the other hand, if there is an average (net) tendency of improvement, an increase in the degree of uncertainty may work in favor of direct intervention. Here, uncertainty reduces the probability of spontaneous recovery, to an extent that the option value effect may be offset. In contrast to this, in standard models of investment under uncertainty this second case is usually ruled out.

In our basic model, based on the assumption that the health state follows a geometric Brownian motion, unambiguous comparative statics results of the treatment costs, the discount rate, and the average rate of change of the patient's health state are obtained. The model can also be extended to allow for risk aversion on the patient's side. Under the (somewhat extreme) assumption that medical intervention eliminates the uncertainty in the development of the patient's health state, watchfully waiting becomes less attractive, as a result. We then proceed to introduce a second type of uncertainty, represented by a Poisson jump process. This captures the possibility of sudden, discontinuous deterioration in the patient's condition. Depending on the extent of deterioration, such an event may make immediate intervention desirable. Even if this is not the case, medical intervention becomes relatively more attractive compared to the model without Poisson jumps, to an extent determined by the parameters of the Poisson process. Generally, the stochastic processes considered here could be adapted to model a wide range of sickness conditions.

In practice, watchfully waiting is often recommended for diseases which are progressing only slowly, and where the benefits of existing therapies are possibly limited. Typical examples are slowly growing cancers (e.g., lymphoma, prostate cancer), which in many cases would not cause severe problems during the patient's lifetime. Furthermore, watchfully waiting is often the preferred approach for dealing with common diseases, such as children's middle ear infections, where many cases resolve spontaneously. Other examples involve inguinal hernia, abdominal aortic aneurysm and mild chronic hepatitis C. Generally, recommendations vary according to the type and severity of illness, and according to the patient's age and willingness to comply with a treatment regime that requires active monitoring.[2]

Although the advantages and weaknesses of the watchfully waiting strategy versus immediate intervention have been assessed for various diseases, most medical studies do not explicitly model the decision process. Moreover, many studies only consider the "static" costs and benefits of the different treatment strategies, such that the option value of waiting is neglected. As mentioned, such a view is myopic and would be appropriate only if any change in the patient's health state came as a complete surprise, in the sense that no probability could be assigned to that event.

In the literature on health economics and medical decision making, there are a few exceptions.[3] In particular, Driffield and Smith (2007) discuss the applicability

[2] References for these examples are: Ardeshna et al. (2003), Bill-Axelson et al. (2005), American Academy of Pediatrics (2004), Fitzgibbons et al. (2006), Valentine et al. (2000) and Wong and Koff (2004).

[3] Decision tree analysis provides another way to avoid the limitations of the static approach, because it requires the treatment decision to be considered at successive decision nodes. In the

of the real options approach to watchfully waiting and consider a trinomial model to describe the progression of a particular disease. At each point in time, there are three decision alternatives - to continue waiting, to treat, or to discharge the patient - and the authors determine the optimal action at each stage. Overall, the analysis by Driffield and Smith is less general than ours in that they only consider a particular example and do not derive comparative statics results. However, it is more general in the sense that discharge is introduced as an explicit decision alternative whereas in our model, waiting is equivalent to not treating the patient.[4]

In an earlier contribution, Whynes (1995) establishes a framework for identifying optimal times of transfer from a watchfully waiting program to direct intervention. Spontaneous resolution of the disease is possible, and its probability is assumed to increase over time according to specific functional forms. As a main result, increases in the probability of self-resolution and in the costs of direct treatment raise the optimal time of transfer, making watchfully waiting more attractive, whereas increases in the monitoring costs and in the probability of disease recurrence have an opposite effect.

Alagoz et al. (2004) and Shechter et al. (2008) are also concerned with the decision when to initiate a therapy. The focus of both papers is on situations where the effectiveness of existing therapies is of limited duration. The considered cases are (living-donor) liver transplantations, where life expectancy with the new organ can be calculated starting from the time of transplantation, and HIV therapy, to which patients often develop resistance over time. The authors assume that the patient's health state evolves according to a discrete Markov process and use clinical data to compute the optimal threshold values for the treatment decision. Under the considered circumstances, delaying treatment may raise the patient's total life expectancy, but the optimal timing also depends on other patient- and disease-related factors.[5]

---

context of watchfully waiting, this type of approach has been applied, e.g., by Katz et al. (1992) and Dietlein et al. (2000). However, this approach is hardly tractable because it requires probability data which is currently not available for most diseases. See also the discussion by Driffield and Smith (2007).

[4] We believe that this is not a serious omission. To our knowledge, complete discharge from watchfully waiting programs is not currently practiced. Nevertheless, it may be optimal for some health states if there are monitoring costs.

[5] Further removed from the concerns of the present paper, Palmer and Smith (2000) and Pertile (2008) apply the theory of investment under uncertainty to study the decision to adopt new health care technologies.

The remainder of the paper is organized as follows. The next section presents the model and describes the method of solution. In Section 4.3, the model is solved under the assumption that the patient's health state evolves continuously according to a geometric Brownian motion. In Section 4.4, we consider the extended model where sudden, Poisson-type shocks to the patient's health state may occur. The scope for applications of the model is discussed in Section 4.5. Finally, Section 4.6 concludes.

4.2 The Model

4.2.1 Assumptions

In this section, we set out the assumptions regarding the development of the illness and the treatment possibilities. There are two economic agents in our model: a physician (he) and a patient (she).

The Patient. We consider a patient who suffers from a particular illness. Her health state at time t is denoted by $h(t) \in [0,1]$, where $h(t) = 1$ represents "good health", $h(t) = 0$ represents death, and time is continuous. For convenience, we will omit the time argument in the following and denote $h(t) = h$ whenever there is no risk of confusion. The patient has a utility function $u(h)$ with the standard properties:

$$u'(h) > 0; \quad u''(h) \leq 0$$

Thus, she is (weakly) risk averse with respect to lotteries over health states. We normalize $u(0) = 0$ and $u(1) = 1$. In the absence of medical intervention, the development of the patient's health state is uncertain, and a central aspect of the model is the choice of a stochastic process with which to characterize this uncertainty. Here, we consider two cases:

Geometric Brownian Motion (GBM). In this case, the development of the patient's health state is described by a geometric Brownian motion with drift rate α

and variance parameter $\sigma > 0$, that is:

$$\frac{dh}{h} = \alpha\, dt + \sigma\, dz$$

The variable z represents a standardized Wiener process, whose increment is normally distributed with mean zero and variance dt. Thus starting from any value $h(t) \in (0,1)$, the patient's condition may have a central tendency of improvement ($\alpha > 0$), stability ($\alpha = 0$), or deterioration ($\alpha < 0$), but its development will also be affected by a random element for the better or worse, to an extent determined by the value of σ. These random changes are uncorrelated over time, and can cumulatively cause the patient's health state to diverge significantly from its central tendency. Moreover, $h = 0$ and $h = 1$ are absorbing states. If reached by the stochastic process, the patient remains there for the rest of the time. Thus, reaching $h = 1$ would be "spontaneous recovery" and $h = 0$ "premature death". This type of process reflects the idea that the patient's health state evolves continuously, and in such a way that there will be no "dramatic" changes within a marginal period of time.

GBM with Poisson Jump Process. In the second scenario, the health state still evolves according to the GBM defined above, but there may also be sudden, discontinuous health shocks whose arrival times follow a Poisson distribution. The stochastic process is described by[6]

$$\frac{dh}{h} = \alpha\, dt + \sigma\, dz + dq$$

where dq denotes the Poisson process. Defining λ as the arrival rate of a Poisson event and ϕ as the rate of deterioration, we assume that:

$$dq = \begin{cases} 0 & \text{with probability } 1 - \lambda\, dt \\ -\phi & \text{with probability } \lambda\, dt \end{cases}$$

Thus at each instant, there is a probability $\lambda\, dt$ that the patient's health state will deteriorate to a value $(1-\phi)\, h(t)$ during the next infinitesimal time interval. We assume that ϕ is a known, positive number, though the model can be generalized to

[6] This type of process was developed by Merton (1976).

allow it also to be a random variable. Moreover, the cases of non-fatal deterioration, where $\phi \in (0,1)$, and sudden death ($\phi = 1$) will be considered separately.

These stochastic processes have been chosen for their simplicity and tractability. Their analytical properties are very well understood. In a general sense they seem to capture quite well the idea of a patient whose health state at a given point in time can be measured, but whose future development is uncertain. Needless to say, however, in any practical application, accurate modeling of the development of the patient's health state would be essential.

The Physician and the Treatment Decision. At any time t, the physician knows the patient's health state, and that it will evolve stochastically according to one of the processes defined above. Whatever the current health state $h \in (0,1)$, a medical intervention (treatment) will restore the patient to good health, but involves a cost c which may be composed of a resource cost and a utility cost (pain, discomfort). We assume that the physician fully internalizes the patient's benefit of the intervention and the total cost, where future costs and benefits are discounted at a rate ρ. We abstract from any agency problems and leave open the question of who pays the resource cost. Of course, the model could also be interpreted in the sense that only the patient's cost share is to be included. Moreover, if the resource cost is met out of government funds, it might be augmented by a shadow price of public expenditure.

A key simplification here is to assume that the intervention restores the patient to good health for the rest of her lifetime. More generally, the treatment outcome might be described as a random variable with a given distribution. This would not change the general nature of our results. Indeed, if the intervention cannot fully restore the patient's health, watchfully waiting and delaying treatment will become even more attractive. Moreover, we could also allow the expected benefit of treatment to be increasing (to some extent) in the patient's health state before the intervention. This will be discussed below.[7]

Time Horizon. In the following, we will solve the model for an infinite time horizon. This has the advantage that time does not enter as a state variable into the problem. Alternatively, we could assume that the patient has a known, finite

[7] For simplicity, we also abstract from any monitoring costs related to watchfully waiting. These could be introduced as a flow cost per time unit, for instance.

lifetime T when in good health. In this case, the treatment decision will indeed become independent of time when the patient's remaining lifetime is long enough.[8] Another possibility is to assume that death arrives stochastically according to a Poisson process. This can be considered as an infinite horizon problem where the discount rate ρ is augmented by the Poisson arrival rate.[9]

4.2.2 Method of Solution

In this section, we define the problem as one of optimal stopping and discuss the method of solution. The analysis is closely related to that of Dixit and Pindyck (1994).

Characterization of the Stopping Problem. As long as there has been no intervention so far, the physician may either continue waiting, in which case the patient gets a flow utility from her current health state, or intervene to obtain the discounted benefit of treatment:[10]

$$\Omega = \int_0^\infty e^{-\rho\tau} d\tau - c = \frac{1}{\rho} - c$$

We assume this value to be positive since treatment would never be optimal otherwise. Technically, we consider an optimal stopping problem, and the optimal time of intervention is chosen according to:

$$\max_t E\left[\int_0^t e^{-\rho\tau} u(h(\tau))\, d\tau + e^{-\rho t}\,\Omega\right]$$

Since the optimal stopping time t^* is stochastic, it cannot be directly determined. Intuitively, we are looking for a threshold value h^*, such that intervention becomes optimal as soon as the patient's health state equals or falls below this value, whereas for $h > h^*$, no treatment will be provided.

8 In Appendix 4.B, we discuss the numerical solution of the finite horizon case and present an example.

9 See, for example, Dixit and Pindyck (1994), pp. 200-201. A reference for the assumption of infinity is Hogan and Walker (2007). The authors consider the choice of education length as an optimal stopping problem and assume that individuals are infinitely lived.

10 Recall intervention restores the patient to good health, $u = 1$.

Lemma 1 *The optimal stopping time t^* is given by $t^* = \inf\{t \,|\, h(t) \leq h^*\}$, where h^* is a threshold value to be determined.*

Dixit and Pindyck (1994) give sufficient conditions to ensure that the optimal stopping time is indeed characterized by Lemma 1.[11] Firstly, in general, the term $u(h) - \rho\,\Omega(h)$, which corresponds to the advantage of waiting versus immediate intervention, must be strictly increasing in h. Here, this is clearly fulfilled since we assume the treatment outcome to be independent of the patient's health state. Secondly, an improvement in the current health state must shift the probability distribution of future health states towards higher values, in the sense of first-order stochastic dominance. This is true for both processes considered in this paper. According to Lemma 1, the continuation (waiting) region is given by $h \in (h^*, 1)$, and the stopping (treatment) region is defined by $h \in (0, h^*]$.

Dynamic Programming Approach. The optimal stopping region can be found using standard techniques of stochastic dynamic programming. Applying the Bellman principle of optimality, the value function takes the form:

$$F(h) = \max\left\{u(h)\,dt + e^{-\rho\,dt}E[F(h')\,|\,h];\,\Omega\right\} \tag{4.1}$$

This function represents the expected present value of benefits when optimal decisions are made from the next marginal time period onward, where $e^{-\rho\,dt}$ is the corresponding discount factor and we define $h' = h(t+dt)$. In the continuation region, the first term in the maximum operator is the larger of the two, implying that the physician will face a similar decision problem in the next period. Multiplying equation (4.1) by $e^{\rho\,dt}/dt$, rearranging, and letting dt go to zero yields

$$\rho\,F(h) = u(h) + \frac{E[dF(h)]}{dt} \tag{4.2}$$

where $E[dF(h)] = E[F(h')\,|\,h] - F(h)$ represents the expected change in the continuation value caused by the stochastic process.

Equation (4.2) can best be understood as an arbitrage condition. The right-hand side is the return per time unit of waiting (i.e., holding the option to make the

[11] See pp. 128-130.

intervention in the future). It consists of the utility derived from the current health state and the expected gain or loss in the option value implied by the stochastic process. The left-hand side is the profit per time unit that the decision maker could - hypothetically - obtain when selling the asset (here, the entitlement to the patient's utility flow) and investing the proceeds at the rate ρ.

Now, we apply Itô's lemma:[12]

$$\frac{E[dF(h)]}{dt} = \alpha F'(h) + \frac{1}{2}\sigma^2 h^2 F''(h) + \lambda \{F[(1-\phi)h] - F(h)\} \tag{4.3}$$

The first two terms correspond to the pure geometric Brownian motion, and the last term reflects the possibility of sudden deterioration caused by the Poisson process. Inserting this expression into equation (4.2), we obtain a differential equation which, together with the boundary conditions, can be solved for the value function $F(h)$. This will be considered more fully below, since the properties of the differential equation crucially depend on the type of the stochastic process.

Boundary Conditions. Since equation (4.2) is valid in the continuation region, where $h \in (h^*, 1]$, we must impose boundary conditions that hold along the interval limits. Regarding the upper boundary, the patient will remain in full health once she has reached $h = 1$. Thus:

$$F(1) = \frac{1}{\rho} \tag{4.4}$$

As the lower boundary is itself unknown, the problem amounts to a free boundary problem. Two more conditions are needed to determine h^* jointly with the value function. Firstly, at the critical health state, the physician must be indifferent between waiting and intervening:

$$F(h^*) = \Omega \tag{4.5}$$

This is the "value-matching" condition. Secondly, the "smooth-pasting" condition requires that the two functions in the Bellman operator meet tangentially at the boundary:

$$F'(h^*) = 0 \tag{4.6}$$

[12] Dixit and Pindyck (1994), Chapter 3, given an introduction. For a more rigorous proof, we refer the reader to Øksendal (2003).

The smooth-pasting condition states that for the threshold level of the health state to be chosen optimally, a small change in h^* must have only second-order effects. In case of an intervention, we gain Ω, but lose the continuation value $F(h)$. Thus, maximization of the expression $\Omega - F(h)$ implies condition (4.6).[13] We can now use equations (4.2)-(4.6) to solve for the optimal threshold value.

4.3 Continuous Disease Progression

Here, we assume that the patient's health state follows the geometric Brownian motion defined above. Before proceeding to the stochastic model, however, we will consider the treatment decision under certainty. Since this is not a static problem, the solution is already relatively complex. Also, it will give us a useful benchmark for the stochastic case. Moreover, to avoid any effects caused by risk aversion, both cases will be analyzed assuming risk neutrality first.

4.3.1 Decision under Certainty

In the deterministic case, the patient's health state evolves according to the function $h(t) = h_0 e^{\alpha t}$. Although the solution of the decision problem may of course be obtained from ordinary calculus, it also arises as a special case of the stochastic model, setting $\sigma = 0$. This is discussed in the Appendix. Here, we concentrate on the economic interpretation.

If the patient's condition has a tendency to deteriorate or remain stable ($\alpha \leq 0$), it is optimal to intervene if the patient's health state equals or falls below the level $\bar{h} \equiv 1 - \rho c$. At the critical health state, the discounted benefit of remaining in the current state forever (h/ρ) just equals the discounted benefit of being in full health ($1/\rho$) minus costs. This kind of decision rule was derived by Jorgenson (1963). It implies that waiting may be beneficial even if there is no uncertainty. That is, if the initial health state h_0 is above the critical value, it is optimal to wait until health has deteriorated to that level. Intuitively, the gain of waiting stems from the fact that the

[13] This equivalence was first mentioned by Samuelson (1965). For a more recent discussion, see Shackleton and Sødal (2005).

treatment costs are discounted over time, which makes early intervention relatively more costly.

If $\alpha > 0$, in contrast, there are no gains to waiting. Instead, it is optimal to intervene immediately or not at all. Even without treatment, the patient will be back in good health at a certain point in time . So the question is whether the benefit from immediate recovery exceeds the costs. Formally, it can be shown that the critical value below which immediate intervention is optimal is implicitly defined by the function

$$\Psi(h;\alpha,\rho,c) = \frac{h}{\rho-\alpha} - \frac{\alpha}{\rho(\rho-\alpha)} h^{\rho/\alpha} - \left(\frac{1}{\rho} - c\right) \tag{4.7}$$

where $\Psi(h^*) = 0$. We can state the following:

Proposition 1 *Under certainty, the threshold value h^* is characterized by*

(i) $\alpha \leq 0: \quad h^* = 1 - \rho c = \bar{h}$

(ii) $\alpha > 0: \quad h^* < 1 - \rho c$

In the second case, the threshold value is a strictly decreasing function of the model parameters α, ρ, and c.

Intuitively, an increase in α leads to accelerated recovery, such that medical intervention will be optimal for a smaller range of health states. As the model properties change with the sign of the drift rate, the function $h^*(\alpha)$ has a kink at $\alpha = 0$ (see Figure 4.2 below). Furthermore, higher treatment costs or steeper discounting of future health gains each reduce the benefits of intervening. These effects will be discussed in more detail in Section 4.3.2.

Waiting Time. We can also express the solution in terms of the optimal stopping time. From the patient's point of view, an important aspect of the healing process is also the waiting time until she is cured - either as a result of treatment or of self-recovery. Overall, an increase in α may prolong the waiting time until treatment (if $\alpha < 0$) or make the treatment region smaller (if $\alpha > 0$), but it will also reduce the waiting time until recovery if this is positive. Remark 1 gives a summary of the waiting times.

Remark 1 *The optimal time of treatment t^* is given by*

(i) $\alpha < 0: \quad t^* = \frac{1}{\alpha} \ln\left(\frac{1-\rho c}{h_0}\right)$ *if* $h_0 > 1 - \rho c$ *and* $t^* = 0$ *otherwise.*

(ii) $\alpha \geq 0: \quad t^* \to \infty$ *if* $h_0 > 1 - \rho c$ *and* $t^* = 0$ *otherwise.*

If $\alpha > 0$ *and* $h_0 > h^*$*, the patient will recover at time* $t^{**} = -(\ln h_0)/\alpha$.

Of course, the assumption of deterministic recovery or deterioration seems quite unrealistic. In the stochastic model, it is not a priori known which of the two boundaries is reached first. Thus, we can expect α to have a non-monotonic effect on the overall waiting time. This will become clear later.

4.3.2 Decision under Uncertainty: Basic Results

In the stochastic case, waiting can be beneficial even if $\alpha > 0$, because the health state may randomly decrease against the positive trend. As mentioned before, there is also an option value of waiting. Intuitively, waiting allows to make a more informed decision in the future. However, uncertainty does not always cause a reduction in the level of treatment, but may sometimes lead to an increase in the optimal threshold value.

Before we can prove these results, we have to establish the basic properties of the solution, in particular, its existence, range and uniqueness. This will be discussed in the following. To begin with, the value function $F(h)$ is derived. Combining equations (4.2) and (4.3), we obtain the following differential equation, for the case without Poisson jumps:

$$u(h) - \rho F(h) + \alpha h F'(h) + \frac{1}{2}\sigma^2 h^2 F''(h) = 0 \tag{4.8}$$

As we assume risk neutrality, for the moment, we set $u(h) = h$. The homogeneous part of equation (4.8) has solutions of the form Ah^{β}, where β is a root of the quadratic equation:

$$\kappa(\beta) \equiv -\rho + \alpha\beta + \frac{\sigma^2}{2}\beta(\beta - 1) = 0 \tag{4.9}$$

The solutions of equation (4.9) are given by

$$\beta_{1/2} = \frac{1}{2} - \frac{\alpha}{\sigma^2} \pm \sqrt{\left(\frac{1}{2} - \frac{\alpha}{\sigma^2}\right)^2 + \frac{2\rho}{\sigma^2}}$$

and have opposite signs. We define β_1 as the positive root and β_2 as the negative one. For later reference, we denote their comparative statics properties:

Lemma 2 *The roots β_1 and β_2 depend on the model parameters as follows:*
(i) $\partial\beta_1/\partial\alpha < 0$ *and* $\partial\beta_2/\partial\alpha < 0$.
(ii) $sign(\partial\beta_1/\partial\sigma) = sign(\alpha - \rho)$ *and* $\partial\beta_2/\partial\sigma > 0$.
(iii) $\partial\beta_1/\partial\rho < 0$ *and* $\partial\beta_2/\partial\rho < 0$.
In particular, we have $\beta_1 \geq 1$ if $\alpha \leq \rho$, and $\beta_1 \leq 1$ if $\alpha \geq \rho$.[14]

Furthermore, it may be verified that

$$F_0(h) = \begin{cases} h/(\rho - \alpha) & \text{if } \alpha \neq \rho \\ (h - h\ln h)/(\rho + \frac{1}{2}\sigma^2) & \text{if } \alpha = \rho \end{cases}$$

are particular solutions of the differential equation (4.8). Thus, the general solution is given by:

$$F(h) = F_0(h) + A_1 h^{\beta_1} + A_2 h^{\beta_2} \tag{4.10}$$

where A_1 and A_2 are constants to be determined. Of course, this represents the continuation value only in the waiting region, whereas in the treatment region, we have $F(h) = \Omega$.

Some remarks are in order here. Firstly, we will not explicitly treat the "special case" $\alpha = \rho$. It is not interesting in itself and also, it may be shown that the solution h^* is a continuous function of α at that point. However, our model differs from most of the literature on investment under uncertainty in that we do consider the case $\alpha > \rho$. This is usually ruled out to prevent the asset value from diverging.[15] Here, such an assumption is not necessary because the health state cannot grow without bounds.

[14] Proof: See Sections 4.A.2-4.A.2.
[15] See, for example, Dixit and Pindyck (1994), Chapter 6.

Now, we can apply the boundary conditions (4.4)-(4.6) to the value function (4.10) in order to determine A_1, A_2 and h^*. The following preliminary result concerns the signs of the two constants:

Lemma 3 *The constant A_2 is always positive. The constant A_1 is positive if $\alpha > \rho$, negative if $\alpha \in [0, \rho)$, and takes ambiguous signs if $\alpha < 0$.*[16]

This can be shown under the assumption that a solution $h^* \in (0,1)$ exists. Intuitively, the value function $F(h)$ has two components. On the one hand, the expression $h/(\rho - \alpha) + A_1 h^{\beta_1}$ represents the discounted benefit of waiting without having the option to intervene. Clearly, this includes the possibility of spontaneous recovery. More precisely, if $\alpha < \rho$, the first term equals the expected discounted utility of future health states, corresponding to a stochastic process without barriers, and the second term represents the expected utility gain or loss due to the presence of the upper absorbing boundary. Using the proof of Lemma 3, it can be shown that the whole expression is positive and increasing in the health state. On the other hand, the term associated with the negative root, $A_2 h^{\beta_2}$, represents the option value related to the medical intervention as such, which is decreasing in the health state. Clearly, treatment becomes less likely as h increases, such that its option value falls.[17] We are now ready to prove the main result of this section.

Proposition 2 *A unique solution for the threshold value h^* exists in the interval $(0, \bar{h})$.*

We first discuss the proof of existence.[18] After eliminating the constants A_1 and A_2 from the equation system (4.4)-(4.6), and after some rearrangement, we obtain the function

$$\begin{aligned}\Phi(h;\alpha,\sigma,\rho,c) \equiv &(1-\beta_1)h^{1+\beta_1-\beta_2} - (1-\beta_2)h \\ &+ (1-\rho c)\left(1-\tfrac{\alpha}{\rho}\right)(\beta_1 h^{\beta_1-\beta_2} - \beta_2) + \tfrac{\alpha}{\rho}(\beta_1 - \beta_2)h^{\beta_1}\end{aligned} \tag{4.11}$$

[16] Proof: See Section 4.A.2.

[17] Note that without the possibility of treatment, the lower boundary would be $F(0) = 0$, such that $A_2 = 0$. A related discussion can be found in Dixit and Pindyck (1994), p. 262.

[18] For a full proof of the proposition, see Section 4.A.3.

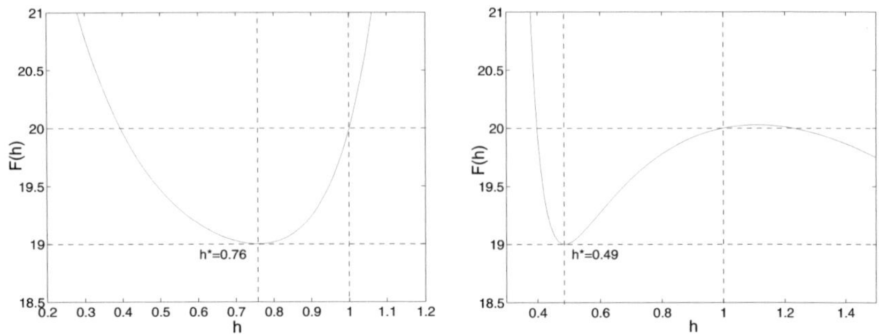

Figure 4.1: Value functions for $\alpha = \pm 0.2$, $\sigma = 0.2$, $\rho = 0.05$, $c = 1$.

which implicitly defines the threshold value by $\Phi(h^*) = 0$. It can be shown that $\Phi(h)$ has opposite signs at the endpoints of the interval $(0, \bar{h})$. As the function is continuous, it must have a root within the open interval. Remember that $\bar{h} = 1 - \rho c$ corresponds to the Jorgenson criterion for the treatment decision under certainty. So if $\alpha \leq 0$, we can also infer that the introduction of uncertainty reduces the level of treatment.

Note that uniqueness is implied by the conditions of Lemma 1. This does not guarantee existence, but if we can find a solution h^*, it must be unique and the value function must be increasing in the interval $(h^*, 1)$. In the Appendix, we also give an explicit proof: Taking the constants A_1 and A_2 as exogenous, the threshold value h^* is unambiguously defined by the boundary conditions. Then, it remains to be shown that the constants are unique.

Finally, it can be shown that the critical value h^* represents a local minimum of the value function or, more precisely, of the "extended" function (4.10) defined for all $h > 0$. There are two cases, and Figure 4.1 shows two representative examples. If $\alpha < 0$ and $A_1 > 0$, the function is globally convex, such that h^* is also a global minimum (left picture). Formally, the second derivative is given by

$$F''(h) = A_1\beta_1(\beta_1 - 1)h^{\beta_1 - 2} + A_2\beta_2(\beta_2 - 1)h^{\beta_2 - 2}$$

which is positive in this case because $\beta_1 > 1$. In the second case, we have either $\alpha < 0$ and $A_1 < 0$, or $\alpha \geq 0$. Together with $A_2 > 0$, this implies that the function value goes to infinity as h tends to zero, and to minus infinity as h tends to infinity.[19] As the function may have at most two extrema, there must be a minimum at h^* and a maximum at some value $h^{**} > 1$ (right picture).

4.3.3 Comparative Statics

How does the solution vary with the model parameters? Our first result concerns the effect of a change in the treatment cost:

Proposition 3 *The optimal threshold value for the treatment decision under uncertainty is strictly decreasing in the treatment cost c.*[20]

As the only effect of a cost increase is to lower the benefit of treatment Ω, the level of treatment must be reduced as well. Thus, the effect is similar to that in the deterministic case.

Since the parameters α, σ and ρ affect the value function via the exponents β_1 and β_2, the analytical comparative statics expressions become difficult to interpret. So we have to rely on numerical simulations to get a clearer picture of the direction and magnitude of the effects. For our central case, we chose the parameter values $\alpha = \pm 0.2$, $\sigma = 0.2$ $\rho = 5\%$ and $c = 1$, as in Figure 4.1 above. We examined a wide range of variations around these values, and the examples discussed below are representative of the general effects.

Claim 1 *The threshold value h^* is a strictly decreasing function of α.*

Here, in contrast to the treatment decision under certainty, an increase in the drift rate lowers the optimal threshold value even if $\alpha \leq 0$. This is because the probability that the patient will spontaneously recover from the disease within a given time interval is always increasing in α. Figure 4.2 illustrates the effect of α under certainty and uncertainty. If only a small amount of uncertainty is introduced ($\sigma = 0.06$), the main consequence will be that the kink in the function $h^*(\alpha)$ is smoothed out. Comparing the threshold value for the deterministic case to our baseline case ($\sigma = 0.2$), we can also infer that the effect of uncertainty may be ambiguous. This can be characterized in more detail:

[19] Note that the term with the highest power, either h or h^{β_1}, has a negative factor.

[20] Proof: See Section 4.A.4.

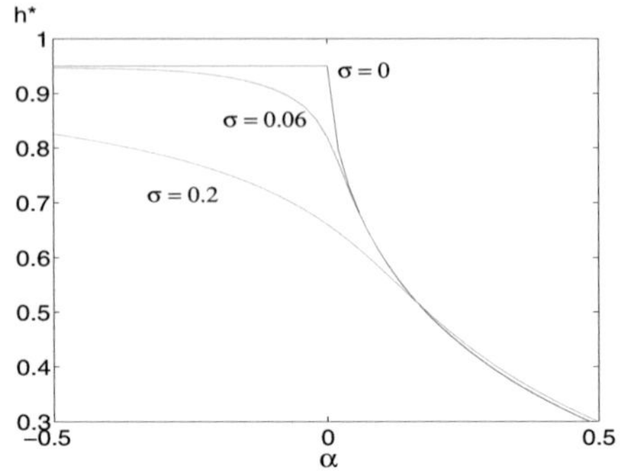

Figure 4.2: Effect of α on h^*.

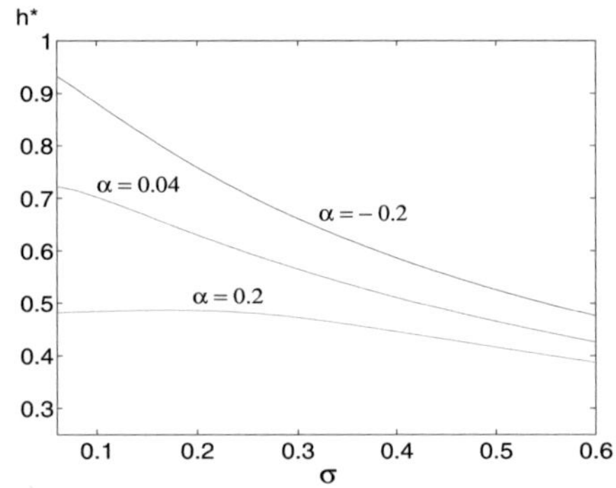

Figure 4.3: Effect of σ on h^*.

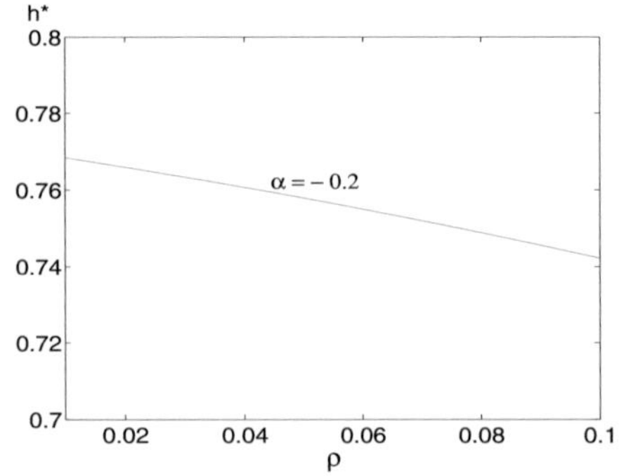

Figure 4.4: Effect of ρ on h^*.

Claim 2 *If $\alpha < \rho$, an increase in the variance term σ has a negative effect on the optimal threshold value h^*. If $\alpha > \rho$, the effect is ambiguous.*

Figure 4.3 illustrates. Two aspects must be considered regarding the effect of σ: On the one hand, an increase in the degree of uncertainty makes waiting more attractive because any new information on the patient's condition - and thus on the relative benefit of treatment - becomes more valuable. This is the option value effect. On the other hand, uncertainty also affects the probability of a spontaneous recovery, and the degree to which this event changes the continuation value of waiting. In the Appendix, we show that in cases where the value function is globally convex, both effects work in the same direction, such that the total effect must be negative. Numerically, the result extends to all cases where $\alpha < \rho$.

In contrast, if the average rate of change in the patient's health state exceeds the discount rate, the second effect may offset the option value effect. Formally, since the positive root β_1 is increasing in σ, the continuation value of waiting is reduced via the term $A_1 h^{\beta_1}$, which is related to spontaneous recovery.[21] Note also that the probability of spontaneous recovery is decreasing in the variance of the stochastic process, as will be discussed below. Overall, the two effects seem to cancel out to a large extent, such that the total effect of uncertainty is quite small in the present case.

Another insight from our analysis is that the effect of uncertainty will be most pronounced if α is close to zero, that is, if the average tendency of the patient's condition is relatively neutral (see Figure 4.2). Here, any new information on the patient's development is especially valuable, so that the option value effect becomes quite important. This result is in line with the fact that watchfully waiting is often recommended for slowly progressing diseases, in particular.

Finally, an increase in the discount rate ρ has a similar effect as in the deterministic case:

Claim 3 *The threshold value h^* is strictly decreasing in the discount rate.*

This is shown in Figure 4.4. Clearly, the effect of ρ on the treatment decision is quantitatively less strong than that of the other model parameters. As mentioned,

[21] The comparative statics expressions are presented in more detail in Section 4.A.4.

the discount rate might also be interpreted to include an exogenous probability of death, driven by a Poisson process. Therefore, we allow it to take relatively high values here.[22]

Probability of Treatment. So far, we have considered the threshold value for the treatment decision as a measure of the level of treatment provided. Depending on the context, the probability of an intervention over a given time period may be a more appropriate measure. For simplicity, we consider the overall probability that the patient's health state reaches the lower boundary h^*. Starting from an initial health state h_0 that lies within the waiting region, this is given by:[23]

$$\pi = \begin{cases} \left(h_0^{1-2\alpha/\sigma^2} - 1\right) / \left((h^*)^{1-2\alpha/\sigma^2} - 1\right) & \text{if } \alpha \neq \sigma^2/2 \\ \ln h_0 \,/\, \ln h^* & \text{if } \alpha = \sigma^2/2 \end{cases}$$

Note that there is zero probability that the health state evolves in the interval $(h^*, 1)$ without ever reaching one of the boundaries. Thus the probability of spontaneous recovery amounts to $1 - \pi$. We can make the following statement:

Remark 2 *The probability of medical intervention is strictly decreasing in α. The effect of σ is negative if $\alpha < 0$, and may be ambiguous if $\alpha > 0$.*

An increase in the drift rate α has straightforward consequences. Taking the lower boundary h^* as given, the probability of reaching this threshold value is reduced, but also, the boundary itself is shifted downwards. These two effects work in the same direction and cause a steep decline in the probability of medical intervention. For the more extreme values of α considered in the analysis, the probability of treatment may be close to zero or one. However, for intermediate values of the drift rate, there is considerable ex ante uncertainty over the necessity of an intervention. Figure 4.5 illustrates the effects of α and σ, assuming an initial health state of $h_0 = 0.9$.

Again, the impact of the variance term is more ambiguous. Taking h^* as given, an increase in σ raises the probability of reaching the *upper* boundary in the case of

[22] Most studies use an equal discount rate of 3-5% for future health gains and costs. See, for example, Brouwer (2005) for a review and critical discussion.

[23] See Dixit (1993) for a derivation.

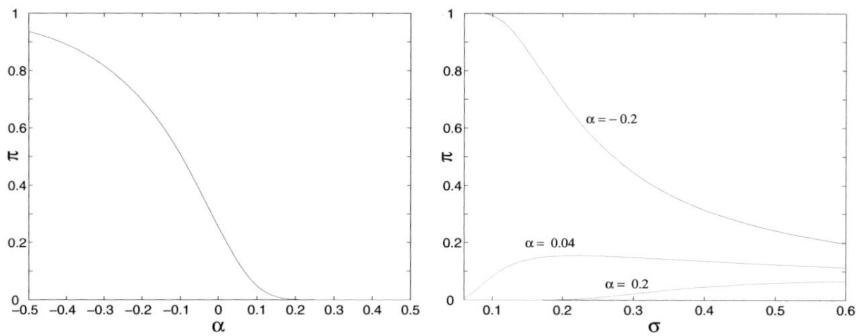

Figure 4.5: Effects of changes in α and σ on the treatment probability.

a negative drift rate. In contrast, if $\alpha > 0$, a deterioration of the patient's health state to h^* becomes more likely. That is, in both cases, the probability that the health state evolves against the central trend is increased. Concerning the total effect of σ, this implies that uncertainty may raise the probability of an intervention even if the threshold value for the treatment decision is reduced.

Expected Waiting Time. For the expected waiting time, a similar intuition applies. That is, although uncertainty reduces the threshold value for the treatment decision if $\alpha < \rho$, this does not necessarily mean that the patient has to wait longer until her condition is resolved.[24]

Here, we consider the expected waiting time until treatment becomes optimal or, alternatively, until the patient recovers from the disease. This is given by:[25]

$$E[t(h \notin (h^*, 1))] = \begin{cases} \left(\ln a - \ln b \dfrac{1 - a^{1-2\alpha/\sigma^2}}{1 - b^{1-2\alpha/\sigma^2}}\right) / \left(\frac{\sigma^2}{2} - \alpha\right) & \text{if } \alpha \neq \sigma^2/2 \\ \ln a (\ln b - \ln a)/\sigma^2 & \text{if } \alpha = \sigma^2/2 \end{cases}$$

[24] Here, it should be mentioned that the possibility of (complete) spontaneous recovery may not be an appropriate assumption for *all* types of diseases where watchfully waiting can be practiced. Instead, it may be possible that the disease stabilizes at a level where treatment is not be desirable. In this case, the patient has to live with an unresolved condition for a longer time.

[25] See Wilmott (2000) for a derivation.

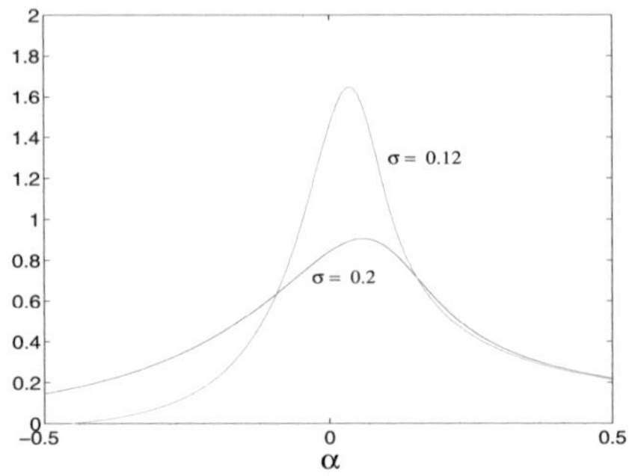

Figure 4.6: Effects of changes in α (and σ) on the expected waiting time.

where $a = h_0/h^*$ and $b = 1/h^*$. Again, the expression is always finite. The following statement applies:

Remark 3 *The expected waiting time reaches a maximum for some intermediate value of the drift rate and decreases as α diverges from that point. The effect of σ is ambiguous and may be negative even if $\alpha < 0$.*

The first part is not surprising. If the drift rate of the stochastic process is close to zero, it will take longer, on average, until one of the boundaries is reached. Here, the development of the patient's health state is mainly driven by the variance term. Therefore, as shown in Figure 4.3.3, an increase in σ reduces the expected waiting time when this is at its highest level. This may also be a general result, although it cannot be proven here.

4.3.4 Generalization to the Case of Risk Aversion

In the following, we show that the main results of Sections 4.3.1 and 4.3.2 can be generalized to the more realistic case of risk aversion. Also, comparative statics results with respect to the degree of risk aversion can be derived.

Assumptions. To keep the analysis as simple as possible, we assume that the patient's preferences are characterized by constant relative and decreasing absolute risk aversion. These properties seem fairly realistic and have have been postulated already by Pratt (1964) and Arrow (1965) in their seminal contributions to the theory of risk bearing. We consider the utility function $u(h) = h^{\theta}$, where $\theta \in (0,1]$. Thus, risk neutrality is incorporated as a special case. The Pratt-Arrow measure of relative risk aversion is given by:

$$r_R(h) = -\frac{u''(h)}{u'(h)}h = 1 - \theta$$

A difficulty of the above utility function is that for health states between zero and one, we always have $h^{\theta} > h$. This inequality implies that a risk averse individual enjoys a higher utility when ill. Generally, the absolute utility level related to a particular health state is increasing in the degree of risk aversion. This "level effect" makes treatment relatively less attractive, which would lead to counter-intuitive results in our context. To avoid these problems, we can simply express the threshold value for the treatment decision in terms of the associated utility level $u(h^*)$. This allows us to bring out the main aspects of the effect treatment decision in a straightforward way.[26]

Results. Again, we consider the decision under certainty first. If $\alpha \leq 0$, the treatment decision remains unchanged in terms of the utility level. That is, medical intervention will be optimal if $u(h) \leq \bar{h}$. As before, the "instantaneous" net present benefit of treatment just becomes positive at this point, whereas for $u(h) > \bar{h}$, this value is negative and treatment can never be optimal.

In contrast, if $\alpha > 0$, the patient's utility in the absence of treatment must be taken into account. Since this is varying over time, a risk averse patient incurs a utility loss due to the concavity of her utility function. As a consequence, medical intervention becomes optimal for higher utility levels than under risk neutrality, and $u(h^*)$ is increasing in the coefficient of relative risk aversion. As mentioned, this result is caused by the change in the health state over time. Here, this cannot be distinguished from the effect of uncertainty.[27]

[26] There is no loss of generality here. We could also normalize the health variable such that h directly reflects a utility level.

[27] The proof for the deterministic case is given in Section 4.A.5.

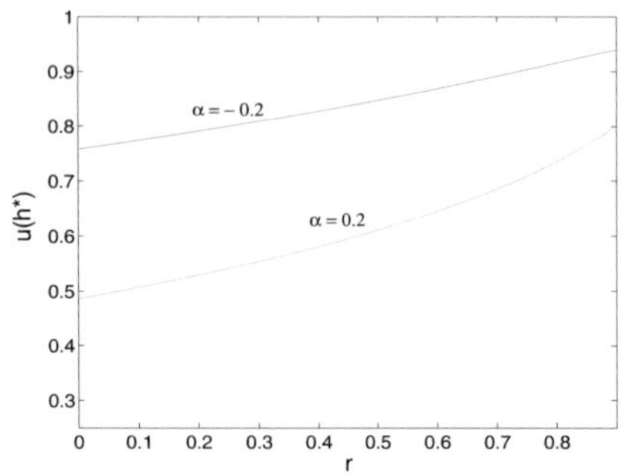

Figure 4.7: Effect of changes in r_R on $u(h^*)$.

For the stochastic case, we first have to prove the existence of a solution. The following statement is a generalization of Proposition 2:

Corollary 1 *Under constant relative risk aversion, a unique solution for the threshold value h^* exists in the interval $(0, \bar{h}^{1/\theta})$.*[28]

The basic properties of the solution are similar to those under risk neutrality. Note that the boundary conditions remain unchanged, as does the homogeneous part of the differential equation (4.8). In contrast, the particular solutions of the differential equation are now given by:

$$F_0(h) = \begin{cases} -h^\theta / [\frac{1}{2}\sigma^2 \theta(\theta - 1) + \alpha\theta - \rho] = -h^\theta / \kappa(\theta) & \text{if } \theta \neq \beta_1 \\ (h^\theta - h^\theta \ln h^\theta)/(\rho + \frac{1}{2}\sigma^2\theta^2) & \text{if } \theta = \beta_1 \end{cases}$$

Generally speaking, the cases $\theta < \beta_1$ and $\theta > \beta_1$ now have to be distinguished. Since risk aversion only affects the patient's flow utility when untreated, the comparative statics are as in the deterministic case:

Claim 4 *The critical utility level $u(h^*)$ below which treatment becomes optimal is increasing in the coefficient of relative risk aversion.*

Figure 4.7 illustrates. A precondition for this result is that medical intervention yields a certain outcome, whereas waiting implies uncertainty. In reality, the treat-

[28] Proof: See Section 4.A.5.

ment outcome may of course be uncertain, as well. However, we conjecture that in most cases, the patient's development will become more predictable after some kind of medical intervention is performed. Thus, the general result is likely to hold if the benefit of the intervention is uncertain.[29]

4.4 Sudden Deterioration of the Health State

So far, we have considered a stochastic process with continuous path. It certainly can be argued that leaving an illness untreated may also bring the possibility of sudden changes, especially for the worse. For example, patients suffering from inguinal hernia face the risk that the hernia may become incarcerated, a problem which usually requires immediate medical attention. Also, patients with abdominal aortic aneurysms face a risk of rupture, which is associated with high mortality rates. However, for small aneurysms, the probability of such an event is low and must be weighed against the risk of surgery. Overall, the model with Poisson jumps seems to capture these situations quite well. We now discuss how this generalization changes our results.

4.4.1 General Model

Generally, two cases can be distinguished. In the first case, medical intervention is always optimal when a sudden deterioration occurs. Thus, a Poisson jump will immediately take the patient's health state to the treatment region. The above examples seem to fit quite well into this description. However, if the rate of deterioration ϕ is low, a single Poisson event will not make immediate intervention necessary. In this sense, the Poisson process can also describe diseases where the patient's condition deteriorates in several steps, followed by periods where no such dramatic changes occur.[30]

[29] Our result is also in line with other studies in the real options literature. For example, Hugonnier and Morellec (2007) find that risk aversion makes early investment more attractive and reduces the option value of waiting. This result is derived in a context of real investment in incomplete markets. See also Henderson and Hobson (2002).

[30] In the real options literature, Poisson processes have been used, in particular, in the context of technology adoption in order to model innovation. From a formal point of view, the models by Farzin et al. (1998) and Murto (2007) are most closely related to ours.

Clearly, the second case is the more general one. Here, we have to distinguish whether intervention remains optimal after the *next* jump, or whether waiting remains superior. Accordingly, the continuation region can be split into two parts: in the lower part, where $h(1-\phi) < h^*$, a jump will end in the stopping region, whereas for $h(1-\phi) > h^*$, the opposite is true. We define the boundary between the two subregions as $\tilde{h} \equiv h^*/(1-\phi)$ and assume that $\phi < 1$. From the discussion in Section 4.2.2, we know that the following differential equation has to be solved:

$$u(h) + \lambda F[(1-\phi)h] - (\rho+\lambda)F(h) + \alpha h F'(h) + \frac{1}{2}\sigma^2 h^2 F''(h) = 0 \qquad (4.12)$$

In the lower part of the continuation region, we have of course $F[(1-\phi)h] = \Omega$. Thus, assuming again risk neutrality, the value function takes the form:

$$F(h) = \frac{\lambda}{\rho+\lambda}\left(\frac{1}{\rho} - c\right) + \frac{h}{\rho+\lambda-\alpha} + A_1 h^{\beta_1} + A_2 h^{\beta_2} \qquad (4.13)$$

Here, the first two terms represent the particular solution for the case $\alpha \neq \rho + \lambda$, and the roots β_1 and β_2 are given by:

$$\beta_{1/2} = \frac{1}{2} - \frac{\alpha}{\sigma^2} \pm \sqrt{\left(\frac{1}{2} - \frac{\alpha}{\sigma^2}\right)^2 + \frac{2(\rho+\lambda)}{\sigma^2}} \qquad (4.14)$$

In contrast, in the interval $(\tilde{h}, 1)$, the value function becomes

$$F(h) = \frac{h}{\rho+\lambda\phi-\alpha} + B_1 h^{\gamma_1} + B_2 h^{\gamma_2} \qquad (4.15)$$

where the special case $\alpha \neq \rho + \lambda\phi$ is omitted, and γ_1 and γ_2 are solutions of the equation:

$$\tilde{\kappa}(\gamma) \equiv -(\rho+\lambda) + \alpha\gamma + \frac{\sigma^2}{2}\gamma(\gamma-1) + \lambda(1-\phi)^{\gamma} = 0 \qquad (4.16)$$

Unfortunately, equation (4.16) has no analytical solution, so that the roots must be determined numerically. However, it is clear that the function $\tilde{\kappa}(\gamma)$ is U-shaped with a positive root γ_1 and a negative root γ_2 (because $\tilde{\kappa}(0) < 0$).

We can now "connect" the two subregions. Denoting the upper part of the value function (4.15) by $G(h)$, we must have:

$$G(\tilde{h}) = F(\tilde{h}); \quad G'(\tilde{h}) = F'(\tilde{h})$$

The first condition requiring continuity is straightforward. According to the second condition, the two branches of the function must meet tangentially at $\tilde{h}$. Intuitively, this is because if no jump occurs, the geometric Brownian motion must cross the boundary $\tilde{h}$ smoothly.[31] Together with the upper boundary, value-matching and smooth-pasting conditions, we can establish an equation system that is to be solved for the four constants and for the threshold value h^*. Then, it has to be verified whether the solution fulfills the condition $h^* < 1-\phi$, such that the upper subregion exists.

In contrast, in the first case mentioned above, a jump will *always* end in the stopping region. A sufficient condition for this case to apply is $h^*_{GBM} > 1-\phi$. That is, the health state after deterioration is so low as to necessitate immediate intervention even if the decision criterion of the GBM model is applied. Intuitively, the threshold value will be higher in the combined model than in the pure GBM model, so we must also have $h^* > 1-\phi$. In the present case, only the lower branch of the value function (4.13) is relevant, which simplifies the model. Clearly, the value function and thus the optimal treatment decision do not depend on the actual rate of deterioration, but only on the arrival rate of a Poisson event. Note, however, that this result depends on the somewhat simplifying assumption that health can be fully restored even if the patient's state momentarily reaches a very low level. Instead, a more complex "recovery function" could be introduced which might change the properties of the solution. However, this would also make the model less tractable.

In principle, we could solve the general model using the described method. However, since the general problem is quite involved, we shall confine ourselves to the following special cases. These bring out the effects of the Poisson parameters λ and ϕ quite well. In particular, the problem is solved for the case where all uncertainty stems from the Poisson process.

[31] We do not show this formally here. Dixit and Pindyck (1994), pp. 130-132, give a proof of smooth-pasting based on a binomial approximation of the stochastic process. This can be applied here as well.

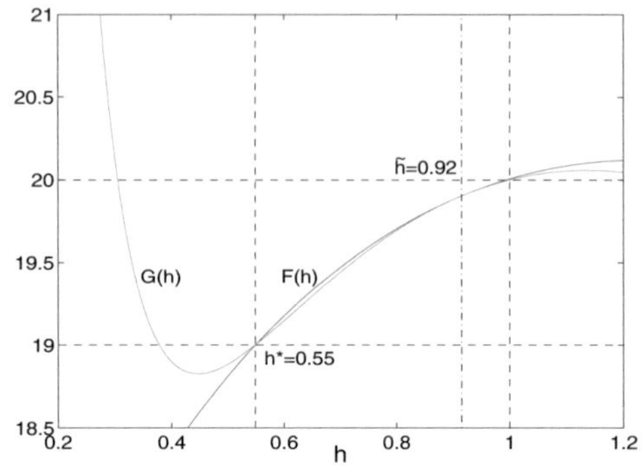

Figure 4.8: Value function for $\alpha = 0.2$, $\sigma = 0$, $\lambda = 0.2$ and $\phi = 0.4$.

4.4.2 Case A: Pure Poisson Uncertainty

Here, we assume that $\sigma = 0$, so that the Poisson process is the only source of uncertainty in the model. If $\alpha > 0$, the above method of solution can be applied. Figure 4.8 shows the two branches of the value function for an example where $1 - \phi > h^*$. Note that the smooth-pasting condition is not relevant if $\sigma = 0$, so that the critical value h^* is not a minimum of the value function.[32]

Figures 4.9 and 4.10 illustrate the comparative statics effects of the parameters of the jump process. Increases in the arrival rate of a Poisson event λ, or in the deterioration rate ϕ have a positive effect on the optimal threshold value. Also, there is a critical value of ϕ above which a further increase in the deterioration rate does not change the treatment decision any longer. Of course, the direction of these effects is not surprising given that the jump process only involves a risk of deterioration.

In contrast, if α is negative, the health state follows a monotonically decreasing process. From the case without Poisson jumps, we know that intervention will be optimal as soon as the patient's health state reaches the Jorgenson threshold level $\bar{h} = 1 - \rho c$. Given that the health shocks are non-lethal ($\phi < 1$), the result and the intuition carry over to the present case.

[32] Intuitively, differentiability is not required at h^*, because the lower boundary can only be crossed by jumping.

The aim of the following example is to give an even stronger justification for the general comparative statics effects.

4.4.3 Case B: Gradual Deterioration

In the limit, the Poisson jump process is described by a process of gradual, deterministic deterioration of the patient's health state. To see this, assume that the jumps arrive infinitely often ($\lambda \to \infty$) and that the jump size becomes infinitesimally small ($\phi \to 0$). Furthermore, let the limiting processes be such that the rate of deterioration is fixed at $\mu \equiv \lambda\phi$. This implies nothing other than a decrease in the drift rate to $\alpha - \mu$. Formally, we can expand the term $\lambda F[(1-\phi)h]$ in equation (4.12) around the point $(1-\phi)h$:[33]

$$\begin{aligned}\lambda F[(1-\phi)h] &= \lambda\left(F(h) - \phi h F'(h) + \frac{1}{2}(\phi h)^2 F''(h) + \dots\right)\\ &= \lambda F(h) - \mu h F'(h).\end{aligned}$$

The second-order term can be ignored (because the factor $\mu\phi$ tends to zero), and the same holds for all terms of higher order. Altogether, equation (4.12) reduces to the differential equation for the geometric Brownian motion, but with α being replaced by $\alpha - \mu$. The GBM model can be applied accordingly.

In conclusion, an increase in μ will raise the threshold value for providing immediate treatment. For the general Poisson jump process, an increase in λ or (possibly) ϕ should have a similar effect.

4.4.4 Case C: Sudden Death

In contrast to the rest of this section, we now assume that $\phi = 1$. Here, the patient may suddenly die from the disease since, by assumption, any medical intervention would come too late. Since waiting can be particularly detrimental in this case, the resulting threshold value h^* will indicate an upper limit on the amount of treatment provided, compared to scenarios with non-lethal health shocks.

[33] See also a related discussion by Murto (2007).

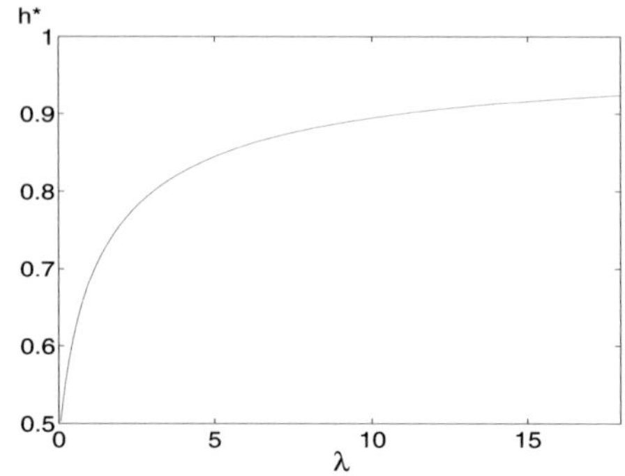

Figure 4.9: Effect of λ on h^*, where $\alpha = 0.2$, $\sigma = 0$, $\phi = 0.4$.

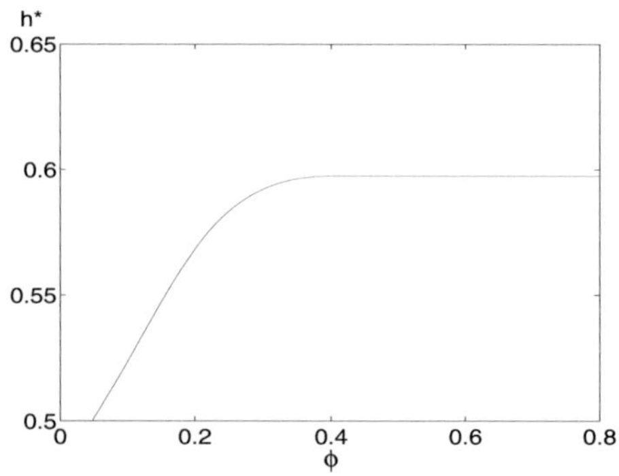

Figure 4.10: Effect of ϕ on h^*, where $\alpha = 0.2$, $\sigma = 0$, $\lambda = 0.4$.

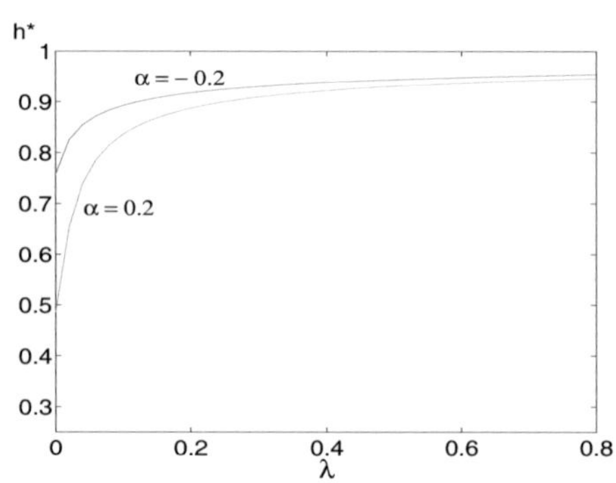

Figure 4.11: Effect of λ on h^*, where $\sigma = 0.2$, $\phi = 1$.

Since we have $F[(1-\phi)h] = 0$, the differential equation (4.12) simplifies to:

$$h - (\rho + \lambda)F(h) + \alpha h F'(h) + \frac{1}{2}\sigma^2 h^2 F''(h) = 0 \qquad (4.17)$$

According to equation (4.17), the Poisson death process corresponds to an increase in the discount rate to $\rho + \lambda$. As mentioned before, this is a standard result. In the present case, however, the discount rate will be back at ρ if the patient reaches good health again. Of course, one might also consider different arrival rates for ill and healthy individuals. More general functional relationships between the current health state and the probability of death could also be assumed.

To solve the present example, we can use our calculations above. In the implicit function (4.11) of the GBM case, the drift rate α is to be replaced by $\alpha - \lambda$, and the roots β_1 and β_2 are as given by equation (4.14). Figure 4.11 illustrates the effect of an increasing arrival rate λ. As can be seen, this causes a steep increase in the threshold level h^* already for relatively low values of λ. Moreover, the threshold level may exceed the Jorgenson level $\bar{h}$. This is because the net present value of treatment Ω is no longer a lower bound for the patient's long-run utility.

4.4.5 Summary

The following statement summarizes the results obtained from the above examples.

Claim 5 *In the model with Poisson jumps, the threshold value h^* is a strictly increasing function of the arrival rate λ. Also, it is strictly increasing in $\phi \in (0,1)$ up to a certain value of the deterioration rate.*

In particular, the limiting result of case B suggests that the statement extends to the more general case where uncertainty is created both by the Poisson process and the geometric Brownian motion.

As mentioned, the Poisson process could be generalized. The aim of the present model was to discuss how the possibility of negative health shocks affects the treatment strategy. If sudden *improvements* in the patient's health state were also possible (such that $\phi < 0$), an increase in the Poisson arrival rate would likely have a different effect. However, the present model seems more relevant for most medical conditions.

Finally, it should be mentioned that there is a discontinuity in our model as ϕ tends to one. As shown above, an increase in the deterioration rate is irrelevant if ϕ is high enough, so that a health shock triggers immediate intervention. In contrast, when the shocks become fatal, the optimal threshold value will discontinuously increase. This is not implausible because there is a natural discontinuity here. To make the model more continuous, however, ϕ could be assumed to be randomly distributed, with a variable probability mass on the event of death.

4.5 Medical Applications

In this section, we discuss the potential applicability of the model to concrete decision situations. Several questions arise in this context: How can the model be adapted to capture the properties of a particular disease? What problems may arise when fitting the model to real-world data? Can the results be translated into practical treatment guidelines? In the following discussion and example, we try to give at least a tentative answer to these questions.

4.5.1 Implementation of the Model

In order to implement the option value approach empirically, we would need data on the progression of the disease. Although in practice the patient's health state can be measured only discretely, it may often be treated as effectively a continuous variable. An example would be the case of abdominal aortic aneurysms, where treatment recommendations are usually based on the size of the aneurysm in millimeters. Similarly, for some types of localized cancer (e.g., renal cell carcinoma, lung cancer), tumor size could be used to measure the progression of the disease and thus the patient's health state.

To avoid any misunderstanding, it should be emphasized that the continuous model has been chosen here because it allows us to analyze the treatment decision at a very general level. However, depending on the measure of the health state, it may be more appropriate to consider a discrete model. For example, it is common practice to use grading or staging systems for different types of cancer. Here, the number of categories of disease progression is rather small, so one could estimate the transition probabilities between the different groups (i.e. this would correspond to a Markov model).

The parameters of the stochastic process (in the present model, α, σ, λ and ϕ) could be estimated from historical case data. For instance, in the case of geometric Brownian motion, maximum likelihood estimation could be used for this purpose. Generally speaking, a good estimator for the drift rate α should be based on a long period of observation, whereas for the estimation of σ, a large *number* of observations is important.[34] The estimation of the model with Poisson jumps would become more problematic. Here, the fact that the health state is measured discretely (and at discrete time intervals) implies that it is hardly possible to distinguish a sudden health shock from a continuous deterioration of the patient's condition. However, if the shocks driven by the Poisson process are clearly defined "emergency events", as in the examples of Section 4.4, only the arrival rate λ must be estimated. This should not cause any particular problems.

Unfortunately, data on the natural history of a disease, that is, on the progression of the disease in the absence of any medical intervention, may be insufficient or unavailable. Although watchfully waiting programs allow these data to be collected, the sample of patients who will not receive treatment will be biased towards relatively mild cases (at least if an effective treatment of the disease exists). This is a general problem in medical decision making. Nevertheless, it must be taken into account when estimating the parameters of the stochastic process.

Generally, an important condition on the measure of the health state is that it must have sufficient prognostic power. In the present context, the health states also need to be ordered in such a way that the optimal stopping region is uniquely defined. That is, in the model, the term $u(h) - \rho\,\Omega(h)$ must be monotonic in h. While we assumed the relative advantage of waiting to be increasing in the health state, there are also cases where the opposite may be true: if the current health state has a strongly positive effect on the expected benefit of treatment, medical intervention will be optimal for relatively favorable health states, whereas watchfully waiting will be preferred when the disease is already quite advanced (such that h is low).

[34] See Campbell, Lo and MacKinlay (1997), Chapter 9, for a more detailed discussion.

However, as in the latter case the chances of curative treatment are relatively small, watchfully waiting corresponds to a very "passive" treatment strategy here.[35]

Regarding the costs and benefits of an intervention, the physician often has to consider a wider range of parameters than assumed in the model. As mentioned, the patient's health state at the time of intervention may affect the expected treatment outcome or the cost of treatment. More generally, factors such as surgery risk or the possibility of disease recurrence have to be taken into account. A central assumption of our model is that these factors can be combined into an estimate of the expected utility of treatment. We conjecture that this is a reasonable approximation in many cases.[36] In practice, monitoring costs related to watchfully waiting must also be taken into consideration.

Finally, data from cost-benefit or cost-effectiveness studies may be applied to determine the optimal threshold value for switching to direct treatment. For instance, in the present model, the threshold value can be expressed in terms of the *relative* benefit of an intervention as $(1-h^*)V/\rho$. Here, the variable V represents the value of a quality-adjusted life year (QALY), and the health state is to be normalized in such a way that the utility of a year of life in the health state h corresponds to the utility of h years of life in good health. Then, treatment becomes optimal if the expected utility gain, based on the patient's current health state, exceeds this threshold value.

If the suggested method is applied, future studies may find that watchfully waiting is beneficial also for patients who, according to current practice guidelines, would receive immediate treatment or, possibly, for illnesses where active monitoring is not currently practiced.[37]

4.5.2 Example

An example of a disease where watchfully waiting is heavily debated in the medical profession is prostate cancer. While it seems evident that delaying direct intervention can be beneficial at least for some patients, there is still an urgent need for

[35] See also the discussion in the next Section 4.5.2.

[36] Alternatively, the patient's health state after treatment might be modeled as a stochastic process as well. This is left for future research.

[37] As discussed above, illnesses with a strong tendency to spontaneous recovery form an exception.

research on the optimal treatment strategy. As will be shown in the following, the real options approach could bring new insight to this issue. The example is illustrative in nature, however, and there is no one-to-one relationship to the theoretical model.

Prostate cancer is one of the leading causes of cancer deaths in men in the Western world. Since the cancer is often slowly growing and mainly affects older men, however, many patients would never be seriously affected by the disease even if untreated. Generally speaking, prostate cancer is not a uniform condition, but there is a high degree of variability in the development of the disease. Current options for treatment, which mainly involve radical prostatectomy and radiotherapy, have significant side effects. For these reasons, watchfully waiting may be superior to immediate intervention for many patients, but it also brings the risk that the cancer may advance so much that treatment becomes less effective.[38]

There is little empirical evidence regarding the costs and benefits of watchfully waiting. For instance, Bill-Axelson et al. (2005) report the results of a controlled trial conducted in Scandinavia, where nearly 700 men were randomly assigned to watchfully waiting or radical surgery between 1989 and 1999. After ten years of follow-up, the disease-specific mortality rate was 14.9% in the first group, compared with only 9.6% in the second group. Radical surgery significantly reduced the disease-specific and overall mortality rate and the risk of metastasis. Neither the costs of treatment nor the option value of waiting were taken into account. An even more important drawback of the study is that most patients had already relatively advanced tumors at the time of diagnosis. Watchfully waiting was generally *not* aimed at providing curative treatment at predefined threshold levels. Instead, these patients received palliative radiation or hormonal therapy more often than the other group.

In recent years, screening examinations for the prostate-specific antigen (PSA) and new biopsy techniques have become available, which allows the discovery of the cancer at a very early stage. This has significantly raised the number of diagnoses. Given that the probability of immediate surgical treatment is still relatively high, there is concern that many of these patients are being overtreated. Clearly, early diagnosis makes watchfully waiting more attractive initially, because it introduces a lead time of several years compared with conventional diagnostic meth-

[38] See Adolfsson (2008) for a survey of the medical literature.

ods.[39] It also allows the provision of treatment at a relatively early stage of the disease even if there is a period of deferral. Against this background, it seems important to define reliable criteria for switching to direct intervention.

Evidence from watchfully waiting programs with the option to provide curative treatment is still missing.[40] In this context, a doubling time of the PSA value of less than two to four years or a progression in the Gleason score, which measures the histological stage of the tumor on a scale of two to ten, to seven or higher have been suggested as threshold values for switching to direct intervention.[41] We believe that the option value approach could be successfully applied to examine whether these criteria are appropriate, or whether they should be amended. It would also be interesting to see how (in an optimizing framework) the introduction of early diagnosis affects the overall probability of surgical intervention. This is not a priori clear in this context.

4.6 Conclusion

We have shown that watchfully waiting represents an important alternative to immediate curative treatment if the course of an illness is uncertain. In the GBM model, an increase in the level of uncertainty raises the benefit of waiting if the patient's condition has a (net) tendency towards deterioration. The gain of waiting is particularly high for slowly progressing diseases. For conditions with a strong tendency to spontaneous recovery however, an increase in the level of uncertainty may work in favor of immediate intervention. Moreover, increases in the drift rate of the stochastic process, in the treatment costs and in the discount rate have a negative effect on the threshold value for the treatment decision. In contrast, the presence of risk aversion or the possibility of sudden shocks to the patient's health state work in favor of immediate intervention.

[39] For instance, initial studies suggest that the disease-specific survival rates at eight years after the first diagnosis are extremely high, ranging from 99 to 100 percent. However, only low-risk patients have been enrolled in the studies. See Adolfsson (2008).

[40] In the medical literature, this strategy is also named "active surveillance", as opposed to the more "traditional" form of watchfully waiting.

[41] See Adolfsson (2008). The Gleason score is a combination of two different scores which each range from one to five. Note that in a more elaborate model, the first measure could be used as an estimate of the rate of change in the patient's condition.

To derive these results, we made several simplifying assumptions. For example, we used rather stylized stochastic processes to characterize the progression of the disease. Furthermore, we assumed the costs and benefits of medical intervention to be independent of the patient's age and health state and of the waiting time until treatment. While these assumptions do not seem very realistic, they are sufficient for our main purpose, which is to analyze the treatment decision at a the most general possible level. Even with a more accurate modeling of the specific characteristics of the illness, the general nature of the results is likely to remain the same.

4.A Proofs

4.A.1 Deterministic Case

Treatment Decision

We start by showing how the threshold value h^* can be obtained from the general stochastic model. By setting $\sigma = 0$, the characteristic equation (4.9) reduces to $\beta = \rho/\alpha$. Assuming $\alpha \neq \rho$, the value function takes the form:

$$F(h) = \frac{h}{\rho - \alpha} + Ah^{\rho/\alpha}$$

In the case $\alpha \leq 0$, the smooth-pasting condition can be rearranged to:

$$Ah^{\rho/\alpha} = -\frac{\alpha h}{\rho(\rho - \alpha)}$$

After inserting A, the value-matching condition simplifies to $h/\rho = 1/\rho - c$. Of course, the upper boundary condition is irrelevant here. If $\alpha > 0$, we solve the upper boundary condition for:

$$A = \frac{1}{\rho} - \frac{1}{\rho - \alpha} = -\frac{\alpha}{\rho(\rho - \alpha)}$$

Inserting this into the value-matching condition yields the implicit function $\Psi(h)$. The smooth-pasting condition is not needed in this case because the lower boundary h^* is never actually reached.

Comparative Statics

We restate the implicit function (4.7), for the case $\alpha > 0$:

$$\Psi(h;\alpha,\rho,c) = \frac{h}{\rho-\alpha} - \frac{\alpha}{\rho(\rho-\alpha)} h^{\rho/\alpha} - \left(\frac{1}{\rho} - c\right) = 0$$

The derivative with respect to the health state is given by:

$$\Psi_h = \frac{1}{\rho-\alpha}\left(1 - h^{\rho/\alpha-1}\right) > 0$$

which is positive because both factors have the same sign. Therefore, the effects of the exogenous variables on h^* take opposite signs as the partial derivatives Ψ_α, Ψ_ρ and Ψ_c.

First, consider a change in α. We have:

$$\Psi_\alpha = \frac{h}{(\rho-\alpha)^2} - \frac{h^{\rho/\alpha}}{(\rho-\alpha)^2} + \frac{h^{\rho/\alpha}}{\alpha(\rho-\alpha)} \ln h > 0$$

Dividing by $h/(\rho-\alpha)^2$ and rearranging yields:

$$h^{(\rho/\alpha-1)} \ln h^{(\rho/\alpha-1)} - h^{(\rho/\alpha-1)} + 1 > 0 \tag{4.18}$$

This holds with equality if $h = 1$. The derivative of the left-hand side with respect to $h \in (0,1)$ is given by $h^{(\rho/\alpha-2)} \ln h^{(\rho/\alpha-1)} (\rho/\alpha - 1)$. This is negative for all $\alpha \neq \rho$, so the inequality must hold at h^*.

The effect of a change in the discount rate is determined by:

$$\Psi_\rho = -\frac{h}{(\rho-\alpha)^2} + \frac{\alpha(2\rho-\alpha)}{\rho^2(\rho-\alpha)^2} h^{\rho/\alpha} - \frac{h^{\rho/\alpha}}{\rho(\rho-\alpha)} \ln h + \frac{1}{\rho^2}$$

Multiplying by $(\rho-\alpha)^2$ yields:

$$-h+\frac{\alpha\,(2\rho-\alpha)}{\rho^2}\,h^{\rho/\alpha}-\left(1-\frac{\alpha}{\rho}\right)h^{\rho/\alpha}\ln h+\left(1-\frac{\alpha}{\rho}\right)^2>0 \tag{4.19}$$

The argument is related to the discussion above. Again, the expression becomes zero at $h=1$. Taking the derivative with respect to h, we just obtain condition (4.18), but multiplied by minus one. Therefore, the left-hand side of (4.19) must be decreasing in $h\in(0,1)$.

Finally, we have $\Psi_c=1$. In conclusion, all three variables have a negative effect on the threshold value h^*.

4.A.2 Stochastic Case: Preliminaries

Properties of β_1 and β_2

Here, we show that $\mathrm{sign}(1-\frac{\alpha}{\rho}\beta_1)=\mathrm{sign}(\rho-\alpha)$ and that $(1-\frac{\alpha}{\rho}\beta_2)$ is always positive.

First Part. We have to determine $\mathrm{sign}(1-\frac{\alpha}{\rho}\beta_1)$ for $\alpha>0$. The expression is (weakly) positive iff:

$$\frac{\rho}{\alpha}+\frac{\alpha}{\sigma^2}-\frac{1}{2}\geq\sqrt{\left(\frac{1}{2}-\frac{\alpha}{\sigma^2}\right)^2+\frac{2\rho}{\sigma^2}} \tag{4.20}$$

This inequality is obtained after inserting β_1, multiplying by ρ/α and rearranging. If the left-hand side is negative, which may occur only if $\rho<\alpha$, there is nothing else to show. If it is positive, the inequality becomes:

$$\begin{aligned}
&\left(\frac{1}{2}-\frac{\alpha}{\sigma^2}\right)^2+\frac{2\rho}{\sigma^2}\geq\left(\frac{\rho}{\alpha}\right)^2+\left(\frac{\alpha}{\sigma^2}-\frac{1}{2}\right)^2+\frac{2\rho}{\alpha}\left(\frac{\alpha}{\sigma^2}-\frac{1}{2}\right)\\
\Leftrightarrow\quad&\left(\frac{\rho}{\alpha}\right)^2-\frac{\rho}{\alpha}\geq 0
\end{aligned}$$

This holds exactly if $\rho\geq\alpha$.

Second Part. We prove that $(1-\frac{\alpha}{\rho}\beta_2)$ is positive for $\alpha<0$. This is equivalent with $|\rho/\alpha|>|\beta_2|$, or:

$$\begin{aligned}
& \frac{1}{2}-\frac{\alpha}{\sigma^2}-\frac{\rho}{\alpha} > \sqrt{\left(\frac{1}{2}-\frac{\alpha}{\sigma^2}\right)^2+\frac{2\rho}{\sigma^2}} \qquad (4.21)\\
\Leftrightarrow \quad & \left(\frac{\rho}{\alpha}\right)^2-\frac{\rho}{\alpha}>0
\end{aligned}$$

which must be true.

Proof of Lemma 2

We consider the effects of the model parameters α, ρ and σ on the roots β_1 and β_2. Below, we can see that the effect of α is always negative, whereas an increase in ρ makes β_1 increase and β_2 decrease.

$$\frac{\partial\beta_{1/2}}{\partial\alpha}=-\frac{1}{\sigma^2}\left(1\pm\left(\frac{1}{2}-\frac{\alpha}{\sigma^2}\right)\sqrt{\left(\frac{1}{2}-\frac{\alpha}{\sigma^2}\right)^2+\frac{2\rho}{\sigma^2}}^{\,-1}\right)<0$$

$$\frac{\partial\beta_{1/2}}{\partial\rho}=\pm\frac{1}{\sigma^2}\sqrt{\left(\frac{1}{2}-\frac{\alpha}{\sigma^2}\right)^2+\frac{2\rho}{\sigma^2}}^{\,-1}$$

The impact of σ is more ambiguous. For convenience, we consider a change in the variance σ^2:

$$\frac{\partial\beta_{1/2}}{\partial(\sigma^2)}=\frac{1}{(\sigma^2)^2}\left(\alpha\pm\frac{1}{\sqrt{\cdot}}\left[\left(\frac{1}{2}-\frac{\alpha}{\sigma^2}\right)\alpha-\rho\right]\right)$$

This expression can be related to the original terms β_1 and β_2:

$$\frac{\partial\beta_1}{\partial\sigma^2}=\frac{-\rho}{(\sigma^2)^2\sqrt{\cdot}}\left(1-\frac{\alpha}{\rho}\beta_1\right)$$

$$\frac{\partial\beta_2}{\partial\sigma^2}=\frac{\rho}{(\sigma^2)^2\sqrt{\cdot}}\left(1-\frac{\alpha}{\rho}\beta_2\right)$$

Based on the results of the last subsection, the derivative of β_1 must be positive if $\alpha>\rho$, and negative if $\alpha<\rho$. Moreover, the derivative of β_2 must be positive.

Proof of Lemma 3

For convenience, we denote the equation system (4.4)-(4.6) in more detail:

$$\frac{1}{\rho-\alpha}+A_1+A_2=\frac{1}{\rho}$$
$$\frac{h}{\rho-\alpha}+A_1h^{\beta_1}+A_2h^{\beta_2}=\frac{1}{\rho}-c$$
$$\frac{1}{\rho-\alpha}+A_1\beta_1h^{\beta_1-1}+A_2\beta_2h^{\beta_2-1}=0$$

Using the upper boundary condition and the smooth-pasting condition to solve for either of the two constants, we obtain:

$$A_1=\frac{1}{\rho-\alpha}\frac{h-\frac{\alpha}{\rho}\beta_2h^{\beta_2}}{\beta_2h^{\beta_2}-\beta_1h^{\beta_1}}; \qquad A_2=\frac{1}{\rho-\alpha}\frac{h-\frac{\alpha}{\rho}\beta_1h^{\beta_1}}{\beta_1h^{\beta_1}-\beta_2h^{\beta_2}}$$

To see that A_2 is always positive, note that the numerator has the same sign as the term $1-\frac{\alpha}{\rho}\beta_1$. That is, it is negative if $\alpha>\rho$ and positive if $\alpha<\rho$. (We have $h^{\beta_1}>h$ in the first case and $h^{\beta_1}<h$ in the second case.) As the denominator of the second term is positive, we have $A_2>0$.

Obviously, A_1 is positive if $\alpha>\rho$. If $\alpha\in[0,\rho)$, equation (4.4) implies that A_1+A_2 must be (weakly) negative, so we have $A_1<0$. For $\alpha<0$, the sign of A_1 is ambiguous. In our numerical example, it is negative only for values of α close to zero. Inserting A_1 and A_2 into the value-matching condition and rearranging yields the implicit function $\Phi(h)$.

4.A.3 Proof of Proposition 2

Existence

We have to show that $\Phi(0)$ and $\Phi(\bar{h})$ have opposite signs. Clearly, the function value

$$\Phi(0)=(1-\rho c)\left(1-\frac{\alpha}{\rho}\right)(-\beta_2)$$

has the same sign as $\rho-\alpha$.

For the second part, we consider the "symmetric" function $\tilde{\Phi}(h) \equiv \Phi(h)h^{\beta_2}$. This has the same sign as $\Phi(h)$ for $h > 0$. At $\bar{h} = 1 - \rho c$, the function value simplifies to:

$$\tilde{\Phi}(\bar{h}) = \left(1 - \frac{\alpha}{\rho}\beta_1\right)\bar{h}^{1+\beta_1} - \left(1 - \frac{\alpha}{\rho}\beta_2\right)\bar{h}^{1+\beta_2} + \frac{\alpha}{\rho}(\beta_1 - \beta_2)\bar{h}^{\beta_1+\beta_2}$$

Case 1. $\alpha > \rho,\ \tilde{\Phi}(\bar{h}) > 0$

We have $\beta_1 < 1$ and $1 - \frac{\alpha}{\rho}\beta_1 < 0$. As $\bar{h}$ is smaller than one, it is clear that $\bar{h}^{1+\beta_1} < \bar{h}^{2\beta_1}$ and $\bar{h}^{1+\beta_2} < \bar{h}^{\beta_1+\beta_2}$. Replace the two smaller terms in $\tilde{\Phi}(\bar{h})$ by the greater ones. Since both terms have a negative factor, the resulting expression is smaller than the initial function, but still positive:

$$\tilde{\Phi}(\bar{h}) > \left(1 - \frac{\alpha}{\rho}\beta_1\right)\left(\bar{h}^{2\beta_1} - \bar{h}^{\beta_1+\beta_2}\right) > 0$$

Case 2. $0 \leq \alpha < \rho,\ \tilde{\Phi}(\bar{h}) < 0$

Here, we have $\beta_1 > 1$ and $1 - \frac{\alpha}{\rho}\beta_1 > 0$. So we can replace $\bar{h}^{1+\beta_2}$ by the smaller term $\bar{h}^{\beta_1+\beta_2}$ to obtain the following comparison:

$$\tilde{\Phi}(\bar{h}) < \left(1 - \frac{\alpha}{\rho}\beta_1\right)\left(\bar{h}^{1+\beta_1} - \bar{h}^{\beta_1+\beta_2}\right) < 0$$

We can conclude that the function $\Phi(h)$ has a root in the interval $(0, \bar{h})$.

Uniqueness

As discussed in the main part, the critical value h^* can be written as a function of the two constants. More precisely, let $h(A_1, A_2)$ be implicitly defined by the boundary conditions on the interval $(0, 1)$. The following proof relies on ideas of Dixit (1989), Appendix A.

Suppose there are two solutions, (A_1, A_2) and (A'_1, A'_2). The value-matching condition can also be expressed as a function of A_1 and A_2:

$$F(A_1, A_2) = \frac{h(A_1, A_2)}{\rho - \alpha} + A_1\, h(A_1, A_2)^{\beta_1} + A_2\, h(A_1, A_2)^{\beta_2}$$

Because of the smooth-pasting condition, we can make an envelope-type argument:

$$\frac{\partial F}{\partial A_1} = h(A_1, A_2)^{\beta_1} \, ; \qquad \frac{\partial F}{\partial A_2} = h(A_1, A_2)^{\beta_2}$$

From condition (4.4), the sum $A_1 + A_2$ must be constant, given the model parameters. Therefore, we have

$$A_1' = A_1 + a \, ; \qquad A_2' = A_2 - a$$

for some number a. Moreover, the two solutions are connected by the line segment $(A_1 + ta, A_2 - ta)$, for $t \in [0,1]$. So we can differentiate $F(\cdot)$ with respect to t rather than A_1 and A_2. Then:

$$\begin{aligned} 0 &= F(A_1', A_2') - F(A_1, A_2) \\ &= a \int_0^1 \left[h(A_1 + ta, A_2 - ta)^{\beta_1} - h(A_1 + ta, A_2 - ta)^{\beta_2} \right] dt \end{aligned}$$

But since $h(A_1, A_2) \in (0,1)$, we have $h(\cdot)^{\beta_1} < 1 < h(\cdot)^{\beta_2}$. This implies that $a = 0$. That is, the solution must be unique.

4.A.4 Comparative Statics

Effect of a Change in the Treatment Cost

The direction of the effect can be proven by totally differentiating the boundary conditions (see Section 4.A.2). From the upper boundary condition, we obtain $dA_2 = -dA_1$. Inserting this into the total differential of the value-matching condition, where $F'(h^*) = 0$, yields $dA_1(h^{\beta_1} - h^{\beta_2}) = -dc$. From the smooth-pasting condition, we obtain:

$$\frac{dh^*}{dc} = \frac{\beta_1 h^{\beta_1 - 1} - \beta_2 h^{\beta_2 - 1}}{F''(h^*)(h^{\beta_1} - h^{\beta_2})} < 0$$

The second derivative is positive at h^*, as well as the numerator. Since $h^* < 1$, we also have $h^{\beta_1} - h^{\beta_2} < 0$.

Effect of a Change in the Variance Term

Totally differentiating the above equation system yields:

$$\frac{\partial h^*}{\partial \sigma^2} = -\frac{(h^{\beta_1} - h^{\beta_2})F_{h\sigma}(h;\sigma) - (\beta_1 h^{\beta_1 - 1} - \beta_2 h^{\beta_2 - 1})F_\sigma(h;\sigma)}{F''(h^*)(h^{\beta_1} - h^{\beta_2})}$$

where we define F_σ and $F_{h\sigma}$ as the partial derivatives of $F(h) \equiv F(h;\sigma)$ and $F'(h) \equiv F_h(h;\sigma)$ with respect to the variance σ^2. These are given by:

$$F_\sigma(h;\sigma) = \left(A_1 h^{\beta_1}\frac{\partial \beta_1}{\partial \sigma^2} + A_2 h^{\beta_2}\frac{\partial \beta_2}{\partial \sigma^2}\right)\ln h$$

$$F_{h\sigma}(h;\sigma) = A_1 h^{\beta_1 - 1}\frac{\partial \beta_1}{\partial \sigma^2}(1 + \beta_1 \ln h) + A_2 h^{\beta_2 - 1}\frac{\partial \beta_2}{\partial \sigma^2}(1 + \beta_2 \ln h)$$

The derivative $\partial h^*/\partial \sigma^2$ has the same sign as the numerator. After inserting F_σ and $F_{h\sigma}$ and rearranging the terms, this becomes:

$$\frac{\partial \beta_1}{\partial \sigma^2} A_1 h^{2\beta_1 - 1} \overbrace{\left[-h^{\beta_2 - \beta_1} + h^{\beta_2 - \beta_1}\ln h^{\beta_2 - \beta_1} + 1\right]}^{+} + \frac{\partial \beta_2}{\partial \sigma^2} A_2 h^{2\beta_2 - 1} \underbrace{\left[h^{\beta_1 - \beta_2} - h^{\beta_1 - \beta_2}\ln h^{\beta_1 - \beta_2} - 1\right]}_{-}$$

Now, we can see that if $\alpha < \rho$ (such that β_1 is decreasing in the variance) and $A_1 > 0$, the effect is clearly negative. These two conditions also imply convexity of the value function. If A_1 is negative, we cannot determine the sign of the total effect analytically. Numerically, the negative part is always dominant. We can also gain intuition on the case $\alpha > \rho$. Here, the positive root β_1 is increasing in the variance. Together with $A_1 > 0$, this creates an ambiguous effect.

4.A.5 Risk Aversion

Decision under Certainty

Under constant relative risk aversion, $u(h) = h^\theta$, the implicit function $\Psi(\cdot)$ can be generalized to the following expression:

$$\Psi(h;\alpha,\rho,c,\theta) = \frac{h}{\rho-\alpha\theta} - \frac{\alpha\theta}{\rho(\rho-\alpha\theta)} h^{\rho/\alpha} - \left(\frac{1}{\rho} - c\right) = 0$$

Now, the partial derivatives with respect to h and θ are given by:

$$\Psi_h = \frac{\theta h^{-1}}{\rho-\alpha\theta}\left(h^{\theta} - h^{\rho/\alpha}\right) > 0$$

$$\Psi_\theta = \frac{\alpha h^{\rho/\alpha}}{(\rho-\alpha\theta)^2}\left(h^{\theta-\rho/\alpha} - h^{\theta-\rho/\alpha}\ln h^{\theta-\rho/\alpha} - 1\right) < 0$$

The threshold value h^* is increasing in θ or decreasing in the degree of risk aversion, which is due to the "level effect" of the utility function. As we are interested in the utility threshold level $u(h^*)$, we define $y = h^{\theta}$. The function Ψ can be rewritten as a function of y. Therefore, the partial derivatives become:

$$\Psi_y = \frac{\theta y^{-1}}{\rho-\alpha\theta}\left(y - y^{\rho/(\alpha\theta)}\right) > 0$$

$$\Psi_\theta = \frac{\alpha y}{(\rho-\alpha\theta)^2}\left(y^{\rho/(\alpha\theta)-1}\ln y^{\rho/(\alpha\theta)-1} - y^{\rho/(\alpha\theta)-1} + 1\right) > 0$$

This implies that $u(h^*)$ is increasing in the degree of risk aversion.

Proof of Corollary 1

We proceed in a similar way as before to obtain the two constants:

$$A_1 = \frac{1}{\kappa(\theta)} \frac{\theta h^{\theta} - \left(\frac{\kappa(\theta)}{\rho} + 1\right)\beta_2 h^{\beta_2}}{\beta_1 h^{\beta_1} - \beta_2 h^{\beta_2}}$$

$$A_2 = \frac{1}{\kappa(\theta)} \frac{\theta h^{\theta} - \left(\frac{\kappa(\theta)}{\rho} + 1\right)\beta_1 h^{\beta_1}}{\beta_2 h^{\beta_2} - \beta_1 h^{\beta_1}}$$

Consequently, the implicit function $\Phi(h)$ is replaced by:

$$\begin{aligned}\Phi(h) =& (\theta-\beta_1)h^{\theta+\beta_1-\beta_2} - (\theta-\beta_2)h^{\theta} \\ &- \tfrac{\kappa(\theta)}{\rho}(1-\rho c)(\beta_1 h^{\beta_1-\beta_2} - \beta_2) + \left(1 + \tfrac{\kappa(\theta)}{\rho}\right)(\beta_1-\beta_2)h^{\beta_1}\end{aligned}$$

Due to the properties of the quadratic equation (4.9), it is straightforward to show that the term

$$\theta - \left(1 + \frac{\kappa(\theta)}{\rho}\right)\beta_1$$

is positive if $\theta < \beta_1$ and negative if $\theta > \beta_1$, and that $\kappa(\theta)$ takes the opposite sign in both cases. Further, the expression

$$\theta - \left(1 + \frac{\kappa(\theta)}{\rho}\right)\beta_2$$

is always positive. Note that these expressions correspond to the terms $1 - \frac{\alpha}{\rho}\beta_{1/2}$ in the case $\theta = 1$. Therefore, the proof of existence of a solution in Section 4.A.3 generalizes to the case of risk aversion if $\bar{h}$ is replaced by $\hat{h}$. (Here, the two cases $\beta_1 < \theta$ and $\beta_1 > \theta$ have to be distinguished.) Furthermore, the value function has similar properties as before, because A_2 remains positive and A_1 is still ambiguous.

4.A.6 GBM with Poisson Jump Process

Case A: Pure Poisson Uncertainty

In the more general case, where $h^* < 1 - \phi$, we have to solve the following system of equations:

$$\begin{aligned}
\frac{1}{\rho + \lambda\phi - \alpha} + B_1 + B_2 &= \frac{1}{\rho} \\
\frac{\lambda}{\rho + \lambda}\left(\frac{1}{\rho} - c\right) + \frac{h}{\rho + \lambda - \alpha} + A h^{\beta} &= \frac{1}{\rho} - c \\
\frac{\lambda}{\rho + \lambda}\left(\frac{1}{\rho} - c\right) + \frac{\tilde{h}}{\rho + \lambda - \alpha} + A \tilde{h}^{\beta} &= \frac{\tilde{h}}{\rho + \lambda\phi - \alpha} + B_1 \tilde{h}^{\gamma_1} + B_2 \tilde{h}^{\gamma_2} \\
\frac{1}{\rho + \lambda\phi - \alpha} + B_1 \gamma_1 \tilde{h}^{\gamma_1 - 1} + B_2 \gamma_2 \tilde{h}^{\gamma_2 - 1} &= \frac{1}{\rho + \lambda - \alpha} + A \beta \tilde{h}^{\beta - 1}
\end{aligned}$$

where $\beta = (\rho + \lambda)/\alpha$. The first two equations represent the upper boundary and value-matching conditions. The last two lines represent the conditions for continuity and differentiability at $\tilde{h}$. After eliminating the three constants, we obtain an implicit equation for h^* of the form

$$k_1\,h^{1+\beta_1-\beta_2}+k_2\,h+k_3\,h^{\beta_1-\beta_2}+k_4+k_5\,h^{\beta_1}=0$$

where:

$$\begin{aligned}
k_1 &= (1-\gamma_1)\left(\frac{1}{\rho+\lambda\phi-\alpha}-\frac{1}{\rho+\lambda-\alpha}\right)-(\gamma_1-\beta)\frac{(1-\phi)^{1-\beta}}{\rho+\lambda-\alpha}\\
k_2 &= -(1-\gamma_2)\left(\frac{1}{\rho+\lambda\phi-\alpha}-\frac{1}{\rho+\lambda-\alpha}\right)+(\gamma_2-\beta)\frac{(1-\phi)^{1-\beta}}{\rho+\lambda-\alpha}\\
k_3 &= \gamma_1\frac{\lambda}{\rho+\lambda}\left(\frac{1}{\rho}-c\right)+(\gamma_1-\beta)\frac{\rho}{\rho+\lambda}\left(\frac{1}{\rho}-c\right)\\
k_4 &= -\gamma_2\frac{\lambda}{\rho+\lambda}\left(\frac{1}{\rho}-c\right)-(\gamma_2-\beta)\frac{\rho}{\rho+\lambda}\left(\frac{1}{\rho}-c\right)\\
k_5 &= (\gamma_1-\gamma_2)\left(\frac{1}{\rho+\lambda\phi-\alpha}-\frac{1}{\rho}\right)(1-\phi)^{-\beta}
\end{aligned}$$

This can be solved numerically.

4.B Finite Time Horizon

Although the assumption of an infinite time horizon is of course unrealistic, it mainly simplifies the model without changing its long-run properties. Here, we assume that the patient has a known, finite lifetime T. It is straightforward to show that this changes the treatment decision only during the last years of her life. In Section 4.B.1, we discuss the structure of the model and the basic results, and in Section 4.B.2, the numerical solution method is presented.

4.B.1 Basic Results

We shall confine ourselves to our basic case, that is, we assume that the patient is risk neutral and that her health state evolves according to the (pure) GBM process. If there has been no intervention up to time t, the discounted benefit of treatment at that time is given by:

$$\Omega(t) = \frac{1 - e^{-\rho(T-t)}}{\rho} - c$$

This value is decreasing over time, and there exists a "critical" time $\hat{t}$ after which treatment will not be efficient anymore. This is defined by:

$$\hat{t} = T + \frac{\ln(1-\rho c)}{\rho}$$

Clearly, $\hat{t}$ is decreasing in ρ and c, and does not depend on the parameters of the stochastic process. In general, the threshold value for the treatment decision will now be time-dependent and must become zero at time $\hat{t}$.

To obtain the free boundary $h^*(t)$ and the value function $F(h,t)$, we have to solve the following partial differential equation (PDE):

$$h(t) - \rho F(h,t) + \alpha h \frac{\partial F(h,t)}{\partial h} + \frac{\sigma^2 h^2}{2} \frac{\partial^2 F(h,t)}{\partial h^2} + \frac{\partial F(h,t)}{\partial t} = 0 \qquad (4.22)$$

This follows from Itô's lemma. Equation (4.22) has no closed-form solution, so we use a finite-difference method to calculate the boundary $h^*(t)$. The general idea is to discretize time as well as the health variable, so that the PDE can be solved via backward iteration. This will be discussed in more detail in the next subsection.

Figure 4.12 illustrates the results for our baseline case with a remaining lifetime of 5 years. The curve $h^*(t)$ separates the treatment region from the waiting region. At the beginning of the considered time period, the threshold value is still at the long-run value corresponding to the infinite case. That is, only a few years before the assumed time of death does the threshold value start to decline. Clearly, due to the end-of-life effect, the probability that there will be an intervention in the future will become quite small as the date $\hat{t}$ draws nearer. It should also be mentioned that the finite decision problem is very similar to the problem of when to exercise a financial option with a given date of expiry.

Of course, medical decisions near the end of life will often be affected by ethical considerations as well. In principle, one might extend the model to allow for the possibility that treatment will be provided to severely ill patients even if it is not

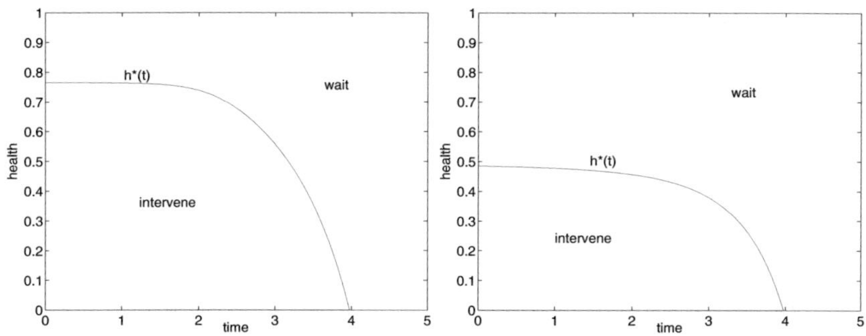

Figure 4.12: Treatment and waiting regions for $T = 5$.

efficient. This is beyond the scope of the present analysis, but might be considered in future research.

4.B.2 Method of Solution

The finite difference method[42] implies that the PDE (4.22) is transformed into a sequence of difference equations which can be solved iteratively. We start by discretizing the variables h and t. So, assume that these can only take the following values:

$$h_i = (i-1)\Delta h \qquad \text{for} \quad i = 1, 2, \cdots, I; \quad h_1 = 0; \quad h_I = 1$$

$$t_j = (j-1)\Delta t \qquad \text{for } j = 1, 2, \cdots, J; \quad t_1 = 0; t_J = T$$

The increments in health (Δh) and time (Δt) can be variably chosen to obtain a more or less fine grid of values. We denote the discretized value function by:

$$f_{i,j} = F(h_i, t_j)$$

[42] See, e.g., Seydel (2006) or Munk (2007) for an introduction.

At each point in time $j < J$, we apply the following boundary conditions:

$$f_{I,j} = \frac{1}{\rho}\left(1 - e^{-\rho(t_J - t_j)}\right)$$
$$f_{1,j} = \max\left\{\frac{1}{\rho}\left(1 - e^{-\rho(t_J - t_j)}\right) - c, 0\right\}$$

In contrast to the infinite model, the free boundary $h^*(t_j)$ cannot be determined *simultaneously* with the value function. Instead, it is appropriate to apply the value-matching condition at the lower boundary $h_1 = 0$. That is, if treatment is optimal for *some* health states at time t_j, the equality $F(h_i, t_j) = \Omega(t_j)$ must hold in the whole treatment region.[43] Also, the smooth-pasting condition cannot be directly imposed, but it will arise endogenously in the numerical model. The next step is to replace the partial derivatives in equation (4.22) by differences. In general, one can use backward, forward or central differences. For the derivative $\partial F/\partial h$, we use the central difference operator

$$D_h f_{i,j} = \frac{f_{i+1,j} - f_{i-1,j}}{2\Delta h}$$

because it often gives a more accurate approximation. The second derivative $\partial^2 F/\partial h^2$ is replaced by:

$$D_h^2 f_{i,j} = \frac{f_{i+1,j} - 2f_{i,j} + f_{i-1,j}}{(\Delta h)^2}$$

Finally, we have to approximate the time derivative $\partial F/\partial t$. There are two alternatives:

$$D_t^- f_{i,j} = \frac{f_{i,j} - f_{i,j-1}}{\Delta t}; \qquad D_t^+ f_{i,j} = \frac{f_{i,j+1} - f_{i,j}}{\Delta t}$$

The first term is the backward difference operator, which is related to the explicit finite difference method. Accordingly, at time $j+1$, equation (4.22) is approximated by:

$$h_i - \rho f_{i,j+1} + \alpha h_i D_h f_{i,j+1} + \frac{\sigma^2 h_i^2}{2} D_h^2 f_{i,j+1} + \frac{f_{i,j+1} - f_{i,j}}{\Delta t} = 0 \qquad (4.23)$$

43 Moreover, our model is stable with respect to the lower boundary condition, in the sense that the results remain nearly unchanged if the condition $f_{1,j} = 0$ is used instead.

Obviously, the function value $f_{i,j}$ can be found by backward induction. However, since the explicit method is not unconditionally stable, we prefer to use the so-called Crank-Nicholson approach, which combines explicit and implicit components.[44] Using the forward difference operator D_t^+, the equivalent of equation (4.22) at time j is

$$h_i - \rho f_{i,j} + \alpha h_i D_h f_{i,j} + \frac{\sigma^2 h_i^2}{2} D_h^2 f_{i,j} + \frac{f_{i,j+1} - f_{i,j}}{\Delta t} = 0 \tag{4.24}$$

This equation corresponds to the (purely) implicit method. Now, we take a weighted average of equations (4.23) and (4.24) with q being the weight on the implicit part, rearrange the terms and multiply by Δt to obtain

$$a_i f_{i-1,j} + b_i f_{i,j} + c_i f_{i+1,j} = \hat{a}_i f_{i-1,j+1} + \hat{b}_i f_{i,j+1} + \hat{c}_i f_{i+1,j+1} - h_i \tag{4.25}$$

where:

$$a_i = \frac{q}{2}\left(\frac{\sigma^2 h_i^2}{(\Delta h)^2} - \frac{\alpha h_i}{\Delta h}\right)\Delta t; \qquad \hat{a}_i = -\frac{1-q}{2}\left(\frac{\sigma^2 h_i^2}{(\Delta h)^2} - \frac{\alpha h_i}{\Delta h}\right)\Delta t$$

$$b_i = -q\left(\rho + \frac{\sigma^2 h_i^2}{(\Delta h)^2}\right)\Delta t - 1; \qquad \hat{b}_i = (1-q)\left(\rho + \frac{\sigma^2 h_i^2}{(\Delta h)^2}\right)\Delta t - 1$$

$$c_i = \frac{q}{2}\left(\frac{\sigma^2 h_i^2}{(\Delta h)^2} + \frac{\alpha h_i}{\Delta h}\right)\Delta t; \qquad \hat{c}_i = -\frac{1-q}{2}\left(\frac{\sigma^2 h_i^2}{(\Delta h)^2} + \frac{\alpha h_i}{\Delta h}\right)\Delta t$$

Equation (4.25) comprises all three methods, with the parameter choices $q = 0$ for the explicit approach, $q = \frac{1}{2}$ for Crank-Nicholson and $q = 1$ for the implicit approach. To obtain the vector $(f_{2,j}, \cdots, f_{I-1,j})$, we have to solve the following system of equations, written in matrix form:

$$\begin{pmatrix} b_2 & c_2 & 0 & \cdots & 0 \\ a_3 & b_3 & c_3 & \ddots & \vdots \\ 0 & \ddots & \ddots & \ddots & 0 \\ \vdots & \ddots & a_{I-2} & b_{I-2} & c_{I-2} \\ 0 & \cdots & 0 & a_{I-1} & b_{I-1} \end{pmatrix} \begin{pmatrix} f_{2,j} \\ f_{3,j} \\ \vdots \\ f_{I-2,j} \\ f_{I-1,j} \end{pmatrix} = \begin{pmatrix} w_{2,j} \\ w_{3,j} \\ \vdots \\ w_{I-2,j} \\ w_{I-1,j} \end{pmatrix} \tag{4.26}$$

[44] The explicit method requires that $2\Delta t \leq (\Delta h)^2$. In practice, this implies that the increment Δh must be relatively large. Moreover, the Crank-Nicholson method often gives a more accurate approximation than the "pure" methods. See, e.g., Seydel (2006).

According to equation (4.25), the vector elements on the right-hand side must take the following values:

$$\begin{aligned}
w_{2,j} &= \hat{a}_2 f_{1,j+1} + \hat{b}_2 f_{2,j+1} + \hat{c}_2 f_{3,j+1} - h_2 - a_2 f_{i,j} \\
w_{i,j} &= \hat{a}_i f_{i-1,j+1} + \hat{b}_i f_{i,j+1} + \hat{c}_i f_{i+1,j+1} - h_i \qquad \text{for } j = 3, \cdots, I-2 \\
w_{I-1,j} &= \hat{a}_{I-1} f_{I-2,j+1} + \hat{b}_{I-1} f_{I-1,j+1} + \hat{c}_{I-1} f_{I,j+1} - h_{I-1} - c_{I-1} f_{I,j}
\end{aligned}$$

In the last two lines, we make use of the boundary conditions given above. It is now clear how the backward iteration works. We have to solve equation (4.26) for every point in time j, where the right-hand side depends on the results of period $j+1$. In the first iteration, we start with the terminal condition $f_{i,J} = 0$. Since equation (4.26) involves a tridiagonal matrix, it can be solved by a well-known algorithm.[45]

Note that the solutions obtained for $f_{i,j}$ correspond to the continuation value of waiting. Before moving from time j to time $j-1$, we have to replace those values of $f_{i,j}$ which are lower than the discounted benefit of treatment by the latter value. In the same step, we can save $h^*(t_j)$ as the highest health state for which treatment is optimal.

[45] See, for example, Seydel (2006), Appendix C.

Chapter 5

Concluding Remarks

In this thesis, I have addressed several questions related to the current debate on reforming the health care sector: Can managed care insurance reduce the costs of medical care while leaving the quality of treatment at least unchanged? What instruments should be employed to prevent risk selection? How can medical decision making be based on more rational criteria? I hope that the answers given in the last chapters offer at least some new perspectives.

At the end of this project, many questions remain unanswered. One can still ask, in a general sense, whether managed care and regulated competition in the health insurance market have the potential to cure the cost disease. Recent experiences in different countries have been somewhat disappointing. In the United States, for example, the introduction of managed care slowed down the growth in health care expenditure, particularly during the 1990s. After the backlash against managed care, however, the growth started to accelerate again. In Germany, some health insurers obtain substantial profits from a favorable risk structure, although the degree of competition, and thus the incentive to make cost reducing investments, is rather small.

Recently, a model of regulated competition in the health insurance sector has been implemented in the Netherlands. The aim is to balance the trade-off between competition and risk selection in a more appropriate way. The reforms are (intended to be) based on suggestions by Enthoven (1978), which are appreciated by many health economists and involve an improved risk adjustment formula as well as the possibility of managed care. It remains to be seen how these policies will perform in practice.

Of course, no country can have a "perfect" health care system. The problems in this sector are very complex, and the political process does not facilitate finding optimal solutions.

Still, I am deeply convinced that health economics can make a significant contribution to the decision making process. To me, it is a fascinating field in its diversity and relevance.

Bibliography

[1] Acemoglu, Daron and Amy Finkelstein (2008). Input and technology choices in regulated industries: Evidence from the health care sector. *Journal of Political Economy*, 116(5), 837Ű880.

[2] Adolfsson, Jan (2008). Watchful waiting and active surveillance: The current position. *British Journal of Urology International* 102(1), 10-14.

[3] Aghion, Philippe and Jean Tirole (1997). Formal and real authority in organizations. *Journal of Political Economy* 105(1), 1-29.

[4] Alagoz, O., L.M. Maillart, A.J. Schaefer and M.S. Roberts (2004). The optimal timing of living-donor liver transplantation. *Management Science* 50(10), 1420-1430.

[5] American Academy of Pediatrics (2004). Diagnosis and management of acute otitis media. *Pediatrics* 113(5), 1451-1465.

[6] Angeles, January and Edwin Park (2009). 'Upcoding' problem exacerbates overpayments to Medicare Advantage Plans. Working Paper, Center on Budget and Policy Priorities.

[7] Ardeshna, K., P. Smith, A. Norton et al. (2003). Long-term effect of a watch and wait policy versus immediate systemic treatment for asymptomatic advanced-stage non-Hodgkin lymphoma: A randomised controlled trial. *The Lancet* 362, 512-522.

[8] Arlen, Jennifer and W. Bentley MacLeod (2005). Torts, expertise and authority: Liability of physicians and managed care organizations. *RAND Journal of Economics* 36(3), 494-519.

[9] Arrow, Kenneth J. (1963). Uncertainty and the welfare effects of medical care. *American Economic Review* 53, 941-973.

[10] Arrow, Kenneth J. (1965). Aspects of the theory of risk bearing. Yrjö Jahnsson Foundation, Helsinki.

[11] Baron, David P. and David Besanko (1984). Regulation, asymmetric information, and auditing. *RAND Journal of Economics* 15, 447-470.

[12] Barros, Pedro P. (2003). Cream-skimming, incentives for efficieny and payment system. *Journal of Health Economics* 22, 419-442.

[13] Baumgardner, James R. (1991). The interaction between forms of insurance contracts and types of technical change in medical care. *RAND Journal of Economics* 22(1), 36-53.

[14] Baumol, William J. (1967). Macroeconomics of unbalanced growth: The anatomy of urban crisis. *American Economic Review* 57(3), 415-426.

[15] Bernheim, B. Douglas and Michael D. Whinston (1985). Common marketing agency as a device facilitating collusion. *RAND Journal of Economics* 16(2), 269-281.

[16] Beck, Konstantin, Maria Trottman, Urs Käser et al. (2006). Nachhaltige Gestaltung des Risikoausgleichs in der Schweizer Krankenversicherung. Ott Verlag, Bern, Switzerland.

[17] Biglaiser, Gary and Ching-to Albert Ma (2003). Price and quality competition under adverse selection: Market organization and efficiency. *RAND Journal of Economics* 34(2), 266-286.

[18] Bill-Axelson, Anna, Lars Holmberg, Mirja Ruutu et al. (2005). Radical prostatectomy versus watchful waiting in early prostate cancer. *New England Journal of Medicine* 352(19), 1977-1984.

[19] Blackwell, David (1951). The comparison of experiments. In: Proceedings of the Second Berkeley Symposium on Mathematical Statistics and Probability. University of California Press, Berkeley, 93-102.

[20] Bolton, Patrick (1987). The principle of maximum deterrence revisited. Working Paper No. 8749, University of California, Berkeley.

[21] Brekke, Kurt R., Robert Nuscheler and Odd Rune Straume (2007). Gatekeeping in health care. *Journal of Health Economics* 26(1), 149-170.

[22] Breyer, Friedrich, Normann Lorenz and Thomas Niebel (2009). Alterung und Gesundheitsausgaben: Ein neuer Test mit RSA-Daten. Working Paper, University of Konstanz.

[23] Brouwer, W., L. Niessen, M. Postma and F. Rutten (2005). Need for differential discounting of costs and health effects in cost effectiveness analysis. *British Medical Journal* 331, 446-448.

[24] Campbell, John Y., Andrew W. Lo and A. Craig MacKinlay (1997). The econometrics of financial markets. Princeton University Press, Princeton, New Jersey.

[25] Chalkley, Martin and James M. Malcomson (1998). Contracting for health services when patient demand does not reflect quality. *Journal of Health Economics* 17(1), 1-19.

[26] Choné, Philippe and Ching-to Albert Ma (2009). Optimal health care contract under physician agency. Working Paper, Boston University.

[27] Cutler, David M., Mark McClellan and Joseph P. Newhouse (2000). How does managed care do it? *RAND Journal of Economics* 31(3), 526-548.

[28] Cutler, David M. and Sarah J. Reber (1998). Paying for health insurance: The trade-off between competition and adverse selection. *Quarterly Journal of Economics* 113(2), 433-466.

[29] Danzon, Patricia M. (1997). Tort liability: A minefield for managed care? *Journal of Legal Studies* 26, 491-519.

[30] Dietlein, M., K. Weber, A. Gandjour et al. (2000). Cost-effectiveness of FDG-PET for the management of solitary pulmonary nodules: A decision analysis based on cost reimbursement in Germany. *European Journal of Nuclear Medicine* 27(10), 1441-1456.

[31] Dixit, Avinash K. (1989). Entry and exit decisions under uncertainty. *Journal of Political Economy* 97(3), 620-638.

[32] Dixit, Avinash K. (1993). The art of smooth pasting. In: J. Lesourne and H. Sonnenschein (Eds.), Fundamentals of Pure and Applied Economics 55. Harwood Academic Publishers, Chur, Switzerland.

[33] Dixit, Avinash K. and Robert S. Pindyck (1994). Investment under uncertainty. Princeton University Press, Princeton, New Jersey.

[34] Dormont, Brigitte, Michel Grignon and Hélène Huber (2006). Health expenditure growth: Reassessing the threat of ageing. *Health Economics* 15, 947-963.

[35] Dranove, David and Kathryn E. Spier (2003). A theory of utilization review. *Contributions to Economic Analysis and Policy* 2(1), Article 9.

[36] Driffield, Tarn and Peter C. Smith (2007). A real options approach to watchful waiting: Theory and an illustration. *Medical Decision Making* 27, 178-188.

[37] Duggan, Mark G. (2002). Does contracting out increase the efficiency of government programs? Evidence from Medicaid HMOs. NBER Discussion Paper No. 9091.

[38] Eggleston, Karen (2000). Risk selection and optimal health insurance-provider payment systems. *Journal of Risk and Insurance* 67(2), 173-196.

[39] Eggleston, Karen (2005). Multitasking and mixed systems for provider payment. *Journal of Health Economics* 24(1), 211-223.

[40] Ellis, Randall P. and Thomas McGuire (1986). Provider behavior under prospective reimbursement: Cost sharing and supply. *Journal of Health Economics* 5(2), 129-151.

[41] Ellis, Randall P. and Thomas G. McGuire (1993). Supply-side and demand-side cost sharing in health care. *Journal of Economic Perspectives* 7(4), 135-151.

[42] Enthoven, Alain C. (1978). Consumer-choice health plan: A national-health-insurance proposal based on regulated competition in the private sector. *New England Journal of Medicine* 298(12), 709-720.

[43] Farzin, Hossein, Kuno Huisman and Peter M. Kort (1998). Optimal timing of technology adoption. *Journal of Economic Dynamics and Control* 22(5), 779-799.

[44] Felder, Stefan and Konstantin Beck (1999). Risikoausgleich und Managed Care. In: Eckhard Knappe (Ed.), Wettbewerb in der Krankenversicherung. Nomos Verlagsgesellschaft, Baden-Baden, Germany.

[45] Fitzgibbons, R.J., A. Giobbie-Hurder, J.O. Gibbs et al. (2006). Watchful waiting versus repair of inguinal hernia in minimally symptomatic men. *Journal of the American Medical Association* 295(3), 285-292.

[46] Frank, Richard G., Jacob Glazer and Thomas G. McGuire (2000). Measuring adverse selection in managed health care? *Journal of Health Economics* 19, 829-854.

[47] Gal-Or, Esther (1997). Exclusionary equilibria in health care markets. *Journal of Economics and Management Strategy* 6(1), 5-43.

[48] Gal-Or, Esther (1999). Mergers and exclusionary practices in health care markets. *Journal of Economics and Management Strategy*, 8(3), 315-350.

[49] Garcia Mariñoso, Begoña and Izabela Jelovac (2003). GP's payment contracts and their referral practice. *Journal of Health Economics* 22(4), 617-635.

[50] Gaynor, Martin (1994). Issues in the industrial organization of the market for physician services. *Journal of Economics and Management Strategy* 3(1), 211-255.

[51] Glazer, Jacob and Thomas G. McGuire (2000). Optimal risk adjustment in markets with adverse selection: An application to managed care. *American Economic Review* 90(4), 1055-1071.

[52] Glazer, Jacob and Thomas G. McGuire (2006). Optimal risk adjustment. In: Andrew M. Jones (Ed.), The Elgar Companion to Health Economics. Edward Elgar, Cheltenham, UK.

[53] Glied, Sherry (2000). Managed Care. In: Anthony J. Culyer and Joseph P. Newhouse (Eds.), Handbook of Health Economics. North Holland, Amsterdam.

[54] Hartwig, Jochen (2008). What drives health care expenditure? Baumol's model of 'unbalanced growth' revisited. *Journal of Health Economics* 27(3), 603-623.

[55] Henderson, Vicky and David G. Hobson (2002). Real options with constant relative risk aversion. *Journal of Economic Dynamics and Control* 27(2), 329-355.

[56] Hogan, Vincent and Ian Walker (2007). Education choice under uncertainty: Implications for public policy. *Labour Economics* 14(6), 894-912.

[57] Hugonnier, Julien and Erwan Morellec (2007). Corporate control and real investment in incomplete markets. *Journal of Economic Dynamics and Control* 31(5), 1781-1800.

[58] Jack, William (2005). Purchasing health care services from providers with unknown altruism. *Journal of Health Economics* 24(1), 73-93.

[59] Jack, William (2006). Optimal risk adjustment in a model with adverse selection and spatial competition. *Journal of Health Economics* 25(5), 908-926.

[60] Jelovac, Izabela (2001). Physicians' payment contracts, treatment decisions and diagnosis accuracy. *Health Economics* 10, 9-25.

[61] Jorgenson, Dale (1963). Capital theory and investment behavior. *American Economic Review* 53(2), 247-259.

[62] Katz, D., B. Littenberg and J. Cronenwett (1992). Management of small abdominal aortic aneurysms: Early surgery vs watchful waiting. *Journal of the American Medical Association* 268, 2678-2686.

[63] Keenan, P.S., M.J. Buntin, T.G. McGuire and J.P. Newhouse (2001). The prevalence of formal risk adjustment in health plan purchasing. *Inquiry* 33, 195-206.

[64] Khalil, Fahad (1997). Auditing without commitment. *RAND Journal of Economics* 28(4), 629-640.

[65] Kifmann, Mathias (2002). Community rating in health insurance and different benefit packages. *Journal of Health Economics* 21, 719-737.

[66] Kifmann, Mathias and Normann Lorenz (2005). Optimal cost reimbursement of health insurers to reduce risk selection. University of Konstanz, Department of Economics, Discussion Paper I - 329.

[67] Kifmann, Mathias and Kerstin Roeder (2008). Can risk-based premiums be more equitable than social insurance? Working Paper, University of Augsburg.

[68] Luft, Harold S. (1999). Why are physicians so upset about managed care? *Journal of Health Policy, Politics and Law* 24(5), 957-966.

[69] Ma, Ching-to Albert (1994). Health care payment systems: Cost and quality incentives. *Journal of Economics and Management Strategy* 3(1), 93-112.

[70] Ma, Ching-to Albert and Thomas G. McGuire (1997). Optimal health insurance and provider payment. *American Economic Review* 87(4), 685-704.

[71] Ma, Ching-to Albert and Michael H. Riordan (2002). Health insurance, moral hazard, and managed care. *Journal of Economics and Management Strategy* 11(1), 81-107.

[72] Malcomson, James M. (2004). Health service gatekeepers. *RAND Journal of Economics*, 35(2), 401-421.

[73] Marchand, Maurice, Motohiro Sato and Erik Schokkaert (2003). Prior health expenditures and risk sharing with insurers competing on quality. *RAND Journal of Economics* 34(4), 647-669.

[74] Mc Donald, Robert L. and Daniel R. Siegel (1986). The value of waiting to invest. *Quarterly Journal of Economics* 106, 707-728.

[75] Melumad, Nahum D. and Dilip Mookherjee (1989). Delegation as commitment: The case of income tax audits. *RAND Journal of Economics* 20(2), 139-163.

[76] Merton, Robert C. (1976). Option pricing when underlying stock returns are discontinuous. *Journal of Financial Economics* 3, 125-144.

[77] Miller, Nolan (2006). Insurer-provider integration, credible commitment, and managed-care backlash. *Journal of Health Economics* 25(5), 861-876.

[78] Miller, R.H. and Harold S. Luft (1997). Does managed care lead to a better or worse quality of care? *Health Affairs* 16(5), 7-25.

[79] Munk, Claus (2007). Introduction to the numerical solution of partial differential equations in finance. Lecture Notes, University of Southern Denmark.

[80] Murto, Pauli (2007). Timing of investment under technological and revenue-related uncertainties. *Journal of Economic Dynamics and Control* 31(5), 1473-1497.

[81] Myerson, Roger B. (1979). Incentive compatibility and the bargaining problem. *Econometrica* 47, 61-63.

[82] Nalebuff, Barry J. and David S. Scharfstein (1987). Testing in models of asymmetric information. *Review of Economic Studies* 54, 265-277.

[83] Newhouse, Joseph P. and Phoebe Lindsey (1988). Do second opinion programs improve outcomes? *Journal of Health Economics* 7(3), 285-288.

[84] Newhouse, J.P., W.G. Manning, E.B. Keeler and E.M. Sloss (1989). Adjusting capitation rates using objective health measures and prior utilization. *Health Care Financing Review* 10(3), 41-54.

[85] Newhouse, Joseph P. (1992). Medical care costs: How much welfare loss? *Journal of Economics Perspectives* 6, 3-21.

[86] Nuscheler, Robert and Thomas Knaus (2005). Risk selection in the German public health insurance system. *Health Economics* 14, 1253-1271.

[87] Øksendal, Bernt (2003). Stochastic differential equations: An introduction with applications (6th Ed.). Springer, Berlin, Heidelberg, New York.

[88] Palmer, Stephen and Peter C. Smith (2000). Incorporating option values into the evaluation of health care technologies. *Journal of Health Economics* 19(5), 755-766.

[89] Pauly, Mark V. (1984). Is cream-skimming a problem for the competitive medical market? *Journal of Health Economics* 3, 87-95.

[90] Pertile, Paolo (2008). Investment in health technologies in a competitive model with real options. *Journal of Public Economic Theory* 10(5), 923-952.

[91] Pindyck, Robert S. (1988). Irreversible investment, capacity choice, and the value of the firm. *American Economic Review* 78, 969-985.

[92] Polsky, Daniel and Sean Nicholson (2004). Why are managed care plans less expensive: Risk selection, utilization or reimbursement? *Journal of Risk and Insurance* 71(1), 21-40.

[93] Pratt, John W. (1964). Risk aversion in the small and in the large. *Econometrica* 32(1), 122-136.

[94] Rosenberg, S.N., D.R. Allen, J.S. Handte et al. (1995). Effect of utilization review in a fee-for-service health insurance plan. *New England Journal of Medicine* 333(20), 1326-30.

[95] Rothschild, Michael and Joseph E. Stiglitz (1976). Equilibrium in competitive insurance markets: An essay on the economics of imperfect information. *Quarterly Journal of Economics* 90(4), 629-649.

[96] Samuelson, Paul A. (1965). Rational theory of warrant pricing. *Industrial Management Review* 6(2), 13-32.

[97] Sappington, David E.M. (1986). Commitment to regulatory bureaucracy. *Information Economics and Policy* 2, 243-258.

[98] Sappington, David E.M. and Tracy R. Lewis (1999). Using subjective risk adjusting to prevent patient dumping in the health care industry. *Journal of Economics and Management Strategy* 8(3), 351-382.

[99] Schlesinger, Mark J., Bradford H. Gray and Krista M. Perreira (1997). Medical professionalism under managed care: The pros and cons of utilization review. *Health Affairs* 16(1), 106-124.

[100] Selder, Astrid (2005). Physician reimbursement and technology adoption. *Journal of Health Economics* 24(5), 907-930.

[101] Seydel, Rüdiger (2006). Tools for computational finance (3rd Ed.). Springer, Berlin, Heidelberg, New York.

[102] Shackleton, Mark B. and Sigbjørn Sødal (2005). Smooth pasting as a rate of return equalization. *Economics Letters* 89(2), 200-206.

[103] Shechter, S.M., M.D. Bailey, A.J. Schaefer and M.S. Roberts (2008). The optimal time to initiate HIV therapy under ordered health states. *Operations Research* 56(1), 20-33.

[104] Shen, Yujing and Randall P. Ellis (2002). How profitable is risk selection? A comparison of four risk adjustment models. *Health Economics* 11(2), 165-174.

[105] Strausz, Roland (1997). Delegation of monitoring in a principal-agent relationship. *Review of Economic Studies* 64, 337-357.

[106] Valentine, R.J., J.D. DeCaprio, J.M. Castillo et al. (1999). Watchful waiting in cases of small abdominal aortic aneurysms - appropriate for all patients? *Journal of Vascular Surgery* 32(3), 441-450.

[107] van Barneveld, Erik, René van Vliet and Wynand van de Ven (1996). Mandatory high-risk pooling: An approach to reducing incentives for cream skimming. *Inquiry* 33, 133-143.

[108] van Barneveld, E., L. Lamers, R. van Vliet and W. van de Ven (2000). Ignoring small predictable profits and losses: A new approach for measuring incentives for cream skimming. *Health Care Management Science* 3(2), 131-140.

[109] van de Ven, Wynand (2006). Response: The case for risk-based subsidies in public health insurance. *Health Economics, Policy and Law* 1(2), 195-199.

[110] van de Ven, Wynand and Randall P. Ellis (2000). Risk adjustment in competitive health plan markets. In: A.J. Culyer and J.P. Newhouse (Eds.), Handbook of Health Economics. North Holland, Amsterdam.

[111] van de Ven, Wynand and Frederik T. Schut (2007). Risk equalization in an individual health insurance market: The only escape from the trade-off between affordability, efficiency and selection. Working Paper, Erasmus University Rotterdam.

[112] van Vliet, René (1992). Predictability of individual health care expenditures. *Journal of Risk and Insurance* 59(3), 443-460.

[113] Whynes, David K. (1995). Optimal times of transfer between therapies: A mathematical framework. *Journal of Health Economics* 14(4), 477-490.

[114] Wickizer, Thomas M. and Daniel S. Lessler (2002). Utilization management: Issues, effects, and future prospects. *Annual Review of Public Health* 23, 233-254.

[115] Wilmott, Paul (2000). Paul Wilmott on quantitative finance (Vol. 1). John Wiley & Sons, Chichester, UK.

[116] Wolff, Nancy and Mark J. Schlesinger (1998). Risk, motives, and styles of utilization review: A cross-condition comparison. *Social Science and Medicine* 47(7), 911-926.

[117] Wong, John B. and Raymond S. Koff (2000). Watchful waiting with periodic liver biopsy versus immediate empirical therapy for histologically mild chronic hepatitis C. *Annals of Internal Medicine* 133(9), 665-675.

[118] Zeckhauser, Richard J.(1970). Insurance, information, and individual action. *Journal of Economic Theory* 2, 10-26.

[119] Zweifel, Peter (2005). The purpose and limits of social health insurance. Working Paper No. 0509, University of Zurich, Socioeconomic Institute.

[120] Zweifel, Peter and Michael Breuer (2006). The case for risk-based premiums in public health insurance. *Health Economics, Policy and Law* 1(2), 171-188.

[121] Zweifel, Peter, Stefan Felder and Markus Meiers (1999). Ageing of population and health care expenditure: A red herring? *Health Economics* 8, 485-496.

LEBENSLAUF

PERSÖNLICHE ANGABEN

Name	Elisabeth Meyer
Geburtsdatum	21. Oktober 1979
Geburtsort	Bad Soden am Taunus
Staatsangehörigkeit	Deutsch

AUSBILDUNG

1989-1997	St.Angela-Schule, Königstein
1997	Abitur
1997-1999	Universität Passau Grundstudium der Volkswirtschaftslehre
1999-2000	Universität Helsinki
2000-2003	Ludwig-Maximilians-Universität München Hauptstudium der Volkswirtschaftslehre Zusatzstudium in Mathematik
2003	Abschluss als Diplom-Volkswirtin
2003-2008	Ludwig-Maximilians-Universität München Promotionsstudium in Volkswirtschaftslehre
2009	Promotion zum Dr. oec. publ.

AKADEMISCHE TÄTIGKEIT

2004-2008	Ludwig-Maximilians-Universität München Seminar für Versicherungswissenschaft Wissenschaftliche Mitarbeiterin

SONSTIGES

1999-2000	Stipendiatin der finnischen Regierung im Rahmen des DAAD-Jahresstipendienprogramms
2003-2006	Stipendiatin Deutsche Forschungsgemeinschaft (DFG), Graduiertenkolleg *Markets, Institutions and the Scope of Government*